JOYCE ROGERS

The
SECRET
of a
WOMAN'S
INFLUENCE

D1515811

BROADMAN PRESS
Nashville, Tennessee

Dewey Decimal Classification: 248.843
Subject Headings: WOMEN - RELIGIOUS LIFE
Library of Congress Catalog Card Number: 88-7338
Printed in the United States of America

Unless otherwise indicated all Scripture quotations are from the
King James Version of the Bible. All Scriptures marked
(NASB) are from the *New American Standard Bible*.
Copyright © The Lockman Foundation, 1960, 1962, 1963,
1968, 1971, 1972, 1973, 1975, 1977. Used by permission.

Library of Congress Cataloging-in-Publication Data
Rogers, Joyce.
   The secret to a woman's influence.
   1. Women—Religious life. I. Title.
BV4527.R639 1988   208'.8042   88-7338
ISBN 0-8054-5069-6

Dedicated

to the women who have
most influenced my life

My dear mother—*Gladys Gentry*
   who first taught me about Jesus and who gave me
   some of the greatest Christian books that most influenced my life,

My sweet mother-in-law—*Rose Rogers*
   who has loved me as a daughter and has given me
   wise counsel,

My godly sister—*Doris Swaringen*
   who has been such an example of unconditional
   love,

My two lovely daughters—who are wise and godly
   homemakers,
      Gayle Foster—who has shared with me her keen
   insight and counsel,
         my special thanks for typing my manuscript and

giving helpful suggestions to make this book possible,

Janice Brock—who has encouraged me with her attitude of praise and enthusiasm,

My two "daughters-in-love"—whom I love as my own,

Cindi Rogers—who has an openness to God's Word that is refreshing and who has opened her heart to me,

Kelly Rogers—who has a listening heart with wise counsel and who has surrounded me with her love,

To godly friends—

Joyce Boatwright and *Johnnie Lord*—whom I have known and loved since college and seminary days,

Juanita Dormer—my "sheltering tree,"

Sarah Maddox and *Velma Rhea Torbett*—who share my vision for women and have helped to bring it to pass,

Dot Clayton and *Virginia Bailey*—who have been with me in the ministry many years and have been like my own flesh and blood,

Buna Sorrell—who has an understanding and wise heart and whom I greatly admire,

Ruth Ann Shelton—who is like a daughter and has greatly ministered to me with her love and artistic talent, and

To my husband's valued secretary—*Linda Glance* whom I love like a daughter, and who has challenged me by her committed life to Christ.

Introduction

As the title implies I have written this book primarily to show the secret of a woman's influence and authority in her Christian life. I have endeavored to examine how this influence roots in the Word of God, the Bible—the reliable, written Word of God—and Jesus Christ—the trustworthy, living Word of God.

They are not identical, but they are inseparable. I would not know about my Savior—neither would you—unless "the Bible tells me so."* But the Bible would be just another history book without the living Word of God interpreting to me its lines.

We will look at Jesus, our supreme example of equality of worth and submission to divine authority. Come, Lord, show us Thyself!

Lord, Show Me Thyself

Lord, show me Thyself
   and may I see
     myself
close beside Thee;

That I may stop
   comparing
my life with
those around me.

Seeing myself
   a little higher
   a little better—

All the time forgetting
   that it's Thee
Who is my Pattern;
   It's Thee
Who I would be like
   Not those around me.

My vision is too low—
   When I look

   d
    o
     w
      n
       w
        a
         r
          d

Surely I can only
   see those
      lower down
         than I.

Lift my eyes upward—
   Fix my eyes
      on Thee.

Lord, show me Thyself
   full of compassion
   full of mercy
   full of grace.

Yes, show me Thyself
   Then I will be
      more like Thee—
         only then!
                    —JR

I will point out that the *extent* and *sphere* of a woman's
ministry are dependent upon ministering under authority

and with the proper priority. A different set of priorities will be explained for the married woman and the single woman. The urgency and primacy of fulfilling the priorities of homemaking and motherhood will be emphasized.

Hopefully, this book will show that God's original plan is not oppressive but holds the secret to true fulfillment and the maximum use of a woman's talents, spiritual gifts, and influence.

In this book I will feature several women from the New Testament and from subsequent history who have used their talents and gifts to influence their world for Christ. At the beginning I would like to honor six modern-day, committed Christian women who have had a profound influence on my own life and ministry to women.

These women have challenged me to keep my priorities as a wife and mother straight, to develop my own gifts, and, in God's proper timing, to channel them to bless others. They are from different parts of God's vineyard, and they have greatly encouraged women to be totally surrendered to Christ and to employ their influence for His glory.

I salute . . .

VONETTE BRIGHT, who first gave me a vision of reaching women for Christ. The wife of Bill Bright, founder of Campus Crusade for Christ, she has motivated thousands of women to help change the conditions of the world through prayer and sharing their faith in the Lord, using the booklet, *The Four Spiritual Laws*.

She is a role model of a wife who is a suitable helper to her husband, complementing him and not competing with him. She has developed her own gifts and ministry after fulfilling her priority assignment to her husband and then to her family.

She has had a worldwide impact through a special emphasis on prayer. She is the founder of The Great Commission Prayer Crusade of Campus Crusade. She is the co-chairman with Pat Boone of The Day of National Prayer, set aside by the President of the U.S. to pray for the leaders of our nation and the welfare of America. In 1984 she chaired The International Prayer Assembly in Seoul, Korea, which gathered 3,000 international Christians dedicated to pray for the world. Her story is in her book, *In Times Like These*.

JILL RENICH MYERS, who challenged me to reach out to meet the everyday needs of women that they might in turn reach out to others. She is the granddaughter of R. A. Torrey and the daughter of missionary parents. After being widowed she is now married to Amos Myers, a preacher of the Gospel.

She founded the organization Winning Women in 1951. Winning Women majors on meeting the needs of women as women, particularly through a biennial retreat ministry. These have grown from fifty-seven to 3,000 in attendance and from one retreat to numerous retreats all over the nation. These retreats feature main speakers and a number of seminars to meet a woman's particular needs. Emphasis is especially placed in the areas of home life, Bible study, prayer, and helping women to experience the reality of Christ's influence.

She has authored a number of books related to the home, including *To Have and to Hold*, translated into several languages, and *Between Us Women*.

JILL BRISCOE, who by example helped me to "give up my right to myself" that I might be released to a larger place of living and ministry. Wife of Stuart Briscoe, pastor, author, and Bible conference leader, she is a dynamic Bible teacher, author, and women's conference speaker. As a young woman she was motivated to "give up her rights" when Stuart was gone ten months out of the year in a Bible-teaching ministry. During those lonely years she stepped out into unusual adventures of faith.

God used those experiences to speak through her to other women going through times of trial. Her husband was then called to the pastorate where she has established a tremendous Bible study and conference ministry to women. Now that her children are grown, she and Stuart frequently travel and speak together in the U.S. and abroad.

Her books include *Prime Rib and Apple, Queen of Hearts, A Time for Living,* and *Here Am I, Send Aaron.*

BEVERLY LAHAYE, who helped give me a burden for the family and for sharing the moral concerns of our day and then becoming involved. She is the wife of Tim

LaHaye, who for years was a pastor, author, and conductor of family life seminars. In 1979 Beverly stepped out on faith and organized Concerned Women of America, which has grown to a membership of over half a million. She has encouraged Christian women to pray and to become involved in moral concerns which deeply affect our families and our nation.

She has actively worked against the passage of ERA, has forthrightly exposed feminism, and has worked against the forces of secular humanism. She has urged CWA supporters to give monetary aid for legal defense to Christians fighting court battles against humanism in the public schools and against legalized abortion.

Her books include: *The Spirit-controlled Woman, How to Develop Your Child's Temperament, and Who But a Woman?*

ELISABETH ELLIOT, who stirred my soul to share the true biblical role of women and to live a truly surrendered life. Now Mrs. Lars Gren, she has been widowed twice. She was first married to Jim Elliot, one of five missionaries martyred by the Auca Indians in Ecuador. Elisabeth won the hearts of the Aucas, and all of Christendom, as she and her five-year old daughter, Valerie, lived among the Aucas and exhibited to them the love and forgiveness of Christ.

She has become a renowned author, first sharing the story of the five martyrs. She has also given a scholarly approach to the biblical roles of men and women and challenges to living sacrificially for Christ and to purity before, and fidelity after, marriage. In her dynamic speaking she lifts up the role of the homemaker to this generation of women.

Her books include: *Shadow of the Almighty, Through Gates of Splendor, Let Me Be a Woman, No Graven Image, Discipline: The Glad Surrender,* and *Love Has a Price Tag.*

DAISY HEPBURN, who motivated me to join together spiritual life growth and moral concerns issues in a ministry to women.

Wife of David Hepburn, director of ministries at Missions Springs Conference Center in Northern California, she is a powerful speaker and motivator of women. Conferences, conventions, women's retreats, radio, and television have carried her across the continent.

She is the founder of Hope of Our Heritage conferences which have had an impact on evangelical Christian women all across the nation. She has also been instrumental in helping churches grow effective women's ministries through stressing a creative and balanced program of spiritual growth and outreach. She is the author of the *Life with Spice* programs and the books, *Why Doesn't Somebody Do Something?* and *Lead, Follow, or Get Out of the Way.*

*Throughout, my main Scriptures are from the King James Version of the Bible, but I have chosen to capitalize the pronouns of Deity.   JR

Contents

The secret of a woman's influence is not equality or self-actualization but a gracious acceptance of a divine assignment in the created order of things.

Joyce Rogers's voice needs to be heard, articulating ancient principles given for the true liberation of both men and women.

—Elisabeth Elliot

Part I

A Woman's Influence

I, as a woman, can have eternal influence. I can make important decisions. When I am loyal, diligent, and trustworthy, I can be delegated vast areas of responsibility. In our home I keep the checkbook, I spend most of the money and buy most of the food, furnishings, and clothing. For thirty-six years I have had the major, daily oversight of our home and of our children. I am a valuable associate to my husband. When I work under his direction I can have a vast amount of influence and authority. I have access to give him counsel if I am wise. I can make him happy and help him to be productive.

I have helped set the values for four children. None of them is perfect, but how I praise God for each of them. They accepted Christ when they were young and are all endeavoring to serve our Lord Jesus Christ. My two daughters, Gayle and Janice, are godly homemakers. My oldest son, Steve, is a minister of music and my son, David, is preparing himself to be a career missionary.

Only God knows the influence of the lullabies and praise songs that I have sung to them. I never sought a separate career, although I've always had extra avenues of service. How I thank God that my two daughters think their highest calling is to be a godly wife and mother. Oh, they are outstanding Bible teachers, have been to college and Bible school, and also have various avenues of service. I trust that the hours I've spent instilling values and just being available to talk has resulted in contented, productive lives.

Yes, sometimes I've been lonely, felt unappreciated, and felt frustrated. But I've never thought I had a second-rate job. It is imminently true that "the hand that rocks the cradle rules the world." Every word that you or I have spoken, every act of love we have performed has had an eternal impact. I believe that my influence has helped my children and indeed others to know and love Jesus Christ. God only knows the power of a woman's influence when she serves *under authority*.

Women of Influence

This past year I have done a study on the lives of the kings of Israel and Judah. I'm not a history "buff" so I can easily get bogged down in too many historical details. I'm a people-oriented person, so I was attracted to the *attitudes, actions,* and *reactions* of the characters of the story. I underlined the different kings and the key passages that indicate the secret to their success or failure. These findings were very interesting.

I especially noticed the names of *women* who had an influence on their sons and husbands. There were some women who influenced their men greatly for *evil*. The names of the wives and mothers were not always mentioned in the historical record, so one should take note when a woman's name appears. Rehoboam's mother was mentioned in 2 Chronicles 12:12, ". . . And his mother's name was Naamah an Ammonitess. (Then it follows:) And he did *evil,* because he prepared not his heart to seek the Lord."

Asa had to remove his mother, Maachah, from being queen because she had made an idol in a grove. Then it was said of King Jehoram of Judah that, ". . . he walked in the way of the kings of Israel, like as did the house of Ahab: *for* he had the *daughter of Ahab to wife:* and he wrought that which was *evil* in the eyes of the Lord" (2 Chron. 21:6, Author's italics throughout).

Then there was King Ahaziah, king of Judah, whose mother Athaliah *"was his counsellor to do wickedly"* (2 Chron. 22:3). What an indictment! And we all know of Jezebel, the wife of Ahab, who plotted *evil* for her husband against Naboth (1 Kings 21:5-15). Oh, the powerful influence of a woman for *evil.*

I don't want *my* name to be mentioned for evil. I want it to be said that my influence was like the mother of King Uzziah, "His mother's name was Jecoliah of Jerusalem, (and it follows:) And he did that which was *right* in the eyes of the Lord." (2 Chron. 26:3*b*,4). Or I want to be like King Lemuel's mother, who taught him the message of Proverbs 31. What an influence for *good* she has been through the ages.

And then there was the influence of a mother on the boy king, Joash. "Joash was seven years old when he began to reign . . . His mother's name was Zibiah of Beersheba. [And it follows] And Joash did that which was *right* in the sight of the Lord." (2 Chron. 24:1-2). "Amaziah was twenty and five years old when he began to reign . . . And his mother's name was Jehoaddan of Jerusalem. [And it follows] And he did that which was *right* in the sight of the Lord" (2 Chron. 25:1-2).

The woman has been used in the Bible to represent good or evil. In the Book of the Revelation it is a *woman,* pictured as *the mother of harlots,* who is portrayed as the epitome of evil (Rev. 17:5). "And the *woman* was arrayed in purple and scarlet colour, and decked with gold and precious stones and pearls, having a golden cup in her hand full of abominations and filthiness of her fornication . . . And I saw the *woman* drunken with the blood of the saints, and with the blood of the martyrs of Jesus" (Rev. 17:4,6).

On the other hand, in Proverbs 8, wisdom is portrayed as a woman who beckons to all that is right and good.

> Doth not wisdom cry? and understanding put forth *her* voice? *She* standeth in the top of high places, by the way in the places of the paths. *She* crieth at the gates, at the entry of the city, at the coming in at the doors. All the words in my mouth are in righteousness; there is nothing froward or perverse in them. Hear instruction, and be wise, and refuse it not (Prov. 8:1-3,8,33).

I want *my* influence to count for *good*—not *evil*. I want my children to rise up and call me blessed and for my husband to praise me (Prov. 31:28). What a joy and reward that will be!

Mary—the Woman Who Has Most Influenced the World

What a woman she must have been! For many years I have been attracted to this "most highly favored woman."

> A woman chosen by God
>   to actually conceive
>   the Son of God;
>   to bear the Son of man
>   to cradle Him in her arms
>   to nurture and train Him
>   and then
>   to give Him up to
>   the whole world!

Evangelical Christians have long neglected the example of Mary, the mother of Jesus, probably because of the overemphasis and even the misrepresentation of the virgin Mary by some. However, she is certainly a role model for any woman who wants to be an influence for God. We will examine how this influence:

- Roots in the Word of God
- Rests in the Will of God
- Releases the Worship of God
- Results in the Word of God

The Word That Was Received

The angel brought a greeting from God, "Hail, thou that art highly favored, the Lord is with thee" (Luke 1:26-28). Or, "Hello, Mary, you're very special to God."

What would be *your* reaction to such a greeting by an angel? I'm sure yours would be the same as Mary's—she was troubled.

> And when she saw him, she was troubled at his saying, and cast in her mind what manner salutation this should be (Luke 1:29).

To relieve her fears he immediately replied,

> Fear not, Mary: for thou hast found favor with God. And, behold, thou shalt conceive in thy womb and bring forth a son, and shalt call His name Jesus. He shall be great, and shall be called the Son of the Highest: and the Lord shall give unto Him the throne of His father David: And He shall reign over the house of Jacob forever; and of His kingdom there shall be no end (Luke 1:30-33).

Mary clearly received a *word from God* through the angel. Probably none of us has had a personal visit from an angel. Mary's was an unusual circumstance, to say the least. But God didn't call on Mary to have *blind faith*. What if He had given her no word and she simply started gaining weight? What if one day she felt movement in her body and finally she delivered a baby? What a frightening experience it would have been. For such an unusual circumstance God sent an unusual messenger. Yes, Mary got a "word from God."

But how are you and I going to receive "a word from God"? Should we expect an angel's visit? For a *virgin birth,* I would say yes! But for *your* circumstances and *my* circumstances, I would answer no! Then *how* does God speak today?

- Through His written Word
- Through sanctified common sense or wisdom
- Through circumstances
- Through the counsel of godly people
- Through the inner voice of the Holy Spirit

I want us to consider especially number one—through His written Word. The *process:*

> I have a need!
> I go to God's Word,
> > seeking God's face
> > through prayer.

One Way:

When I am in a regular, consistent study of God's Word, God then applies His Word to my situation.

Example:

My son David was overseas as a missions volunteer on Operation Mobilization's missionary ship, the *Doulos.* I was naturally concerned for his welfare—physically, emotionally, and spiritually.

In my daily study of God's Word I was reading Psalm 25. Verses 12 and 13 said, "What man is he that feareth the Lord? him shall he teach in the way that he shall choose. His soul shall dwell at ease." In the center column the "note" stated, ". . . *shall lodge in goodness.*" When I read that, God strongly spoke to my heart and used that phrase, *lodge in goodness,* to visualize for me that David was actually dwelling in God's goodness, even though he was a half a world away. I cannot convince you that God spoke to me in my spirit. But *I* know, for such a peace flooded my soul! I had known in my mind that God was watching over my son. But His Word had been made real to my spirit by His Spirit. God's "word" to me that day is still vivid in my heart today.

Another Way:
   A *Subject Study* concerning a specific need in my life. *Examples:*

> I have a need for guidance.
> I have a need for strength and comfort.
> I have a need for healing, and the like.

I remember one particular time in my life when I needed strength and comfort. I looked up the words strength and comfort in my concordance and read all the verses listed. The ones God particularly "spoke to my heart" I "shaded" with a colored pencil. I am using another Bible now, but I can still look through my old Bible and quickly find those verses God gave to me during that time of need. They are "shaded" in purple.

On another occasion I had a deep need for guidance. I did a *subject study* on the Holy Spirit. I shaded those verses with a yellow pencil. These studies made a profound impact on my life as I studied the subject in which I had a great need.

God will speak to us in our times of need if we are

diligent to seek Him with our whole hearts and to "study to show ourselves approved unto Him."

Least Desirable Way:

The *"lucky dip"* method—just open God's Word and put your finger on a verse. If you're desperate, I don't say that God can't speak to you this way. But we could be easily deceived using this approach.

Don't *force* a *"word"* if God doesn't deeply impress. We can just convince ourselves instead of receiving a "word from God." If we think God speaks to us through His Word, take that "word" and *Wait* on God. *Test it!* Seek His face concerning that "word" and what it means. Don't read into verses what is not there.

Learn to recognize the difference between the promises that are the great principles of God's Word and specific promises given to specific people. Sometimes a specific word also contains a great all-time principle. We must "rightly divide" the Word of God (2 Tim. 2:15).

Now back to the virgin Mary! Why do you think she so easily received God's word to her? I believe she had a *prepared heart.* Luke 1:28 and 30 say that she was "highly favored." I like what the center column reference in my Bible says this means: Graciously Accepted!

God had been observing Mary.

> He knew *who* she was—
> He called her name.
> He knew *what* she was—
> He knew she was a virgin.

Mary was one of five women in the genealogy of Jesus in Matthew 1:1-17. The forgiveness and love of God extended to:

> Tamar—a victim of incest
> Rahab—a harlot
> Bathsheba—an adulteress
> Ruth—a heathen.

But for *this* task, God had to have a *virgin*. And Mary was a virgin. Not that Mary was *sinless* as some have declared her to be, for in verse 46 she herself said, "My spirit has rejoiced in God, my *Savior*." But Mary *was* a virgin—a virgin with a heart for God. She had a heart already prepared to receive this word when it came.

To receive a "word from God," *you* and *I* must have a *prepared heart,* or why should God speak to us? Let's ask ourselves some questions.

- What's the condition of my heart?
- If God were to give me a "word," would I be prepared to hear it?
- Would I even know that He spoke to me?

Mary could have said to her mother, "Say, did I have a crazy dream last night! I dreamed an angel spoke to me. You'll never believe what he said to me. Isn't that the funniest thing you ever heard?" Mary obviously *knew* the promises concerning the Messiah. Mary obviously *believed* the promises concerning the Messiah: because she didn't ask why. She had only one question, an honest question! How? "*How* shall this be, seeing I know not a man?"

Most of us would have asked why. "Why me, Lord?" Isn't that the first question we usually ask when some earth-shaking experience happens to us? "Why, why, Lord? Why did this happen to me? I just don't understand! If I only understood why, then I could handle it."

Haven't you asked that of God? Oh, *I* have! Many times. If not verbally, my *heart* cried it out. A memorable exception stands out in my life when I didn't ask why. Thirty years ago when my little baby, Philip, was suddenly taken into the presence of God, I didn't cry out, "Oh God, why, why me?" No, instead I asked how. "How should I deal with this deep grief in my life? What should I do now?"

I've wondered in years since then why there was such victory in the midst of such grief? That may have been part of the secret. I gave up my "right to understand." A song that helped me do that is entitled, "We'll Talk It Over" by Ira Stanphill. I sang it over and over again.

> Though shadows deepen
>   And my heart bleeds
> I will not question
>   The way He leads
> This side of heaven
>   We know in part
> I will not question
>   A broken heart
>
> Chorus:
> We'll talk it over
>   in the bye and bye
> We'll talk it over

> my Lord and I
> I'll ask the reasons
> He'll tell me why
> When we talk it over
> in the bye and bye.
>
> I'll hide my heartache
> behind a smile
> And wait for reasons
> til afterwhile
> And though He try me
> I know I'll find
> That all my burdens
> are silverlined.[1]

I still visualize that private talk Jesus and I will have one day in heaven when "I shall know even as I am known." I have not always been that wise, and I have not always been that victorious.

Now Mary had a honest question, "*How* can this be, seeing I know not a man?" God, through the angel Gabriel, gave her an honest answer. What an answer it was. What a word from God! "For with God, *nothing* shall be impossible." Some things God *wants* us to understand, but He never wants us to question His love, His wisdom, and His judgment.

- Is your heart prepared?
- Have you invited Him to be Lord of your life?
- Are you seeking to please Him?

Seek ye first the kingdom of God and all these things shall be added unto you (Matt. 6:33).

Is your heart willing? Willing to leave the question why with God and only seek how you can deal with that "word" He brings into your life?

The Will That Was Relinquished

It was God's will for the virgin Mary to conceive in her womb a son by the Holy Ghost—

to be called Jesus
who would not be the son of Joseph
but the Son of the Highest
the very Son of God!

This was God's will for her life! Did she have any choice in the matter? Yes, she did! "And Mary said, behold the handmaid of the Lord; be it unto me according to thy word." In other words, "Yes, Lord! I'm *available* to do your will, just like You said. I deliberately choose—by faith in Your word—to enter into Your will for my life," but *she* had to choose His will for her life.

Talk about "freedom of choice." This generation has distorted God's original design for "freedom of choice." Today many claim that it means freedom to kill or not to kill your unborn child. God indeed gave us the freedom to choose right or wrong. However, we will be accountable for our choices.

Free to Choose

She was *free to choose*
to do His will or not;
Free to live a normal life

To marry Joseph
to bear *his* sons
and daughters.

But she was also *free to choose*
to give her body
yielded to His will;
Yes, to bear a Son
Who bore the likeness
of His Heavenly Father.

She was *free to choose*—
to reject God's invitation
to maintain her reputation
to forget the angel's salutation
to ignore mankind's salvation!

But she was also *free to choose*
a life of full submission
according to His Word
a faith in God
in Whom all things
are possible.

She was *free to choose*
and so are we
God, take *my* life
and overshadow me
with Your dear Spirit.
Be born in me today—and grow

I'm yielded to Your will,
"Be it unto *me* according
to Your Word."

—JR

Do you know God's will for *your* life? First, you must
receive a "word from God." Then you must *choose* that

will for you, by faith in His Word. This is called submission.

> Submission to the will
> of Him Who guides me still
> Is surety of His love revealed
> My soul shall rise above
> This world in which I move,
> I conquer only where I yield.
> —C. Austin Miles[2]

This generation of upbeat women, who have called themselves feminists, look upon this word as demeaning. But ladies, in this *word* lies one of the secrets of becoming a great influence for God. A synonym for submission is *meekness*. And just think of the blessings God has promised the meek.

> Blessed are the meek, for they shall inherit the earth (Matt. 5:5).

> The meek will He guide in judgment, and the meek will He teach His way (Ps. 25:9).

The Worship That Was Released

Many years ago I discovered how trusting Jesus, the *living* Word of God, joined with the *written* Word of God, releases the worship of God. Sometimes worship is simply a natural overflow of your life—something you *feel* like doing.

> But whether we feel like it
> or whether we don't feel like it—
> We *must* worship God!

It is our highest calling. It is an expression of our faith in God.

When did Mary worship? *Before* the performance came (*see* Luke 1:45). She *had* believed (past tense). There *shall be* a performance (future tense). In Mary's eyes it was already done. "He that is mighty *hath* done (past tense) to me great things; and holy is His name" (Luke 1:49).

Have *you* learned to worship God? Let me share a little more from one of my life's experiences; for it was a "crash course" in Christian living for me. I refer to the death of my baby thirty years ago. One of the wonderful lessons I learned out of that experience was how to worship God. I said earlier that one of the secrets of victory is not questioning God—not asking *why* but *how*. A part of the *how* is to respond with an attitude of worship, praising God by faith when we don't *feel* like it.

I don't like hypocrisy. If I didn't *feel* like praising God, I wasn't going to *fake* it. "Fakey" praise doesn't communicate victory and it won't produce it. It will only produce a "sick grin."

During that experience I learned to "faith my praise" to God. The *basis* of this concept is found in God's *written* Word—the Bible. The *power* for performing this *act of faith* is found in God's *living* Word—Jesus Christ. I went to God's Word to seek help. He led me to what I needed. A few examples are the following verses:

> The Lord gave and the Lord hath taken away: blessed be the name of the Lord (Job 1:21).

I will bless the Lord at all times: His praise shall contin-
ually be in my mouth (Ps. 34:1).

Because Thy lovingkindness is better than life, my lips
shall praise Thee. Thus will I bless Thee. I will lift up
my hands unto Thy name (Ps. 63:3-4).

These verses taught me by command and example
that I should praise God at *all* times, even in the midst of
trouble. I didn't merely give mental assent to these
"words from God's Word." I obeyed and put them into
practice on a daily basis.

At first it was difficult to learn to praise by faith. In my
spirit He showed that if I could not originate words of
praise on my own, that I was welcome to use His
words—words from God's Word, the Bible. He would
teach me to praise. Indeed He did, and I experienced the
reality of His promises. Today I can say with all the feeling of my soul—*His* lovingkindness is indeed better than
life itself.

The Work That Has Resulted

The angel didn't stay and hold Mary's hand. He didn't
come back every night to reassure her. "And the angel
departed from her" (Luke 1:38*b*). She was left with only
a word from God. She had to hold onto that. Someone
has said, "Don't doubt in the dark what God has shown
you in the light."

God also gave a "word" to Joseph, assuring him of
Mary's genuine love and commitment to him. God is not
unreasonable in His demands (see Matt. 1:19-20). Then

to Mary, who believed God's promises, came the day when the performance was accomplished.

> Blessed is she that believed: for there shall be a performance of those things which were told her from the Lord (Luke 1:45).

And indeed there was!

One "silent night" in the little town of Bethlehem a baby was born.

> A Baby—a Baby was born!
> He would save His people
>   from their sins.
>
> A Baby—A Baby was born!
> But He was *born to die*
>   for the sins of
>   all mankind.

Do *you* have a "word from God"? Has your "angel" left and you are holding only a "word from God"? Are you believing God?

I'm holding onto some "words from God" in behalf of my children, my husband, my friends, and those I'm ministering to. I've dated them in my Bible. I review them from time to time, memorize them, believe them, claim them—remind God about them!

Recently, after many years, I saw a "performance" of one of those "words from God." Indeed, it has been worth all the prayer, all the concern, all the faith, all the time invested in believing God's Word and praising Him while I waited on Him to *deliver* what He had promised me.

The influence of Mary will be felt through all eternity. How grateful I am that a young virgin maiden had so prepared her heart that she heard God's Word; that she believed God's Word.

A Small Intruder

No wedding feast
  No loved ones gathered;
No friends to laugh and sing
  Instead an angel's greeting,
You're special, Mary
  You'll be the mother of the King.

No honeymoon, no ecstasy
  of young love's sweet demand
Instead a quiet questioning:
  "How can this be when
I know not a man?"

Not much time alone with Joseph
  to plan, to dream
    to love
Instead a "small Intruder"
  sent with a message
    from above.

No sad disappointment
But His divine appointment
  with young Mary,
    lass of Galilee
Instead a dedication
And a joyful adoration
  Here, Lord, is my availability!

—JR

God only knows the influence my life or your life can be if we will hear and believe God's word to us and say, "Yes, Lord, I'm available!"

The Privilege and Influence of Being a Mother

This generation has demeaned motherhood and confused young women as to the importance of this role. But how grateful I am that for thirty-four years I have had the privilege of being a mother. I cannot begin to tell you how many hours I've spent holding my babies next to my breast, singing to them and telling them how *I* loved them and how *Jesus* loved them. I didn't keep an account of the hours I spent reading to them from the Bible and other books about the Bible. I remember when my oldest son, Steve, was only two years old, his favorite Bible story was the arrest of Jesus in the Garden of Gethsemane.

I also don't know how many hours I've spent carpooling and making trips to piano lessons. And God only knows the hours I've spent in prayer, talking to my Heavenly Father about my children. I postponed taking voice and piano lessons. There wasn't time or money for me to add them to the list. Although I wrote a few things and filed them in a drawer, I never had time even to give a thought that one day I might write a book. Many days were so mundane that I forgot to think about what an influence I was having on the world. You see, greatness is built from the blocks of daily faithfulness to the task at hand.

There is a description of the King's daughter in Psalm

45. It says that she is all glorious within and that her clothing is interwoven with gold. Then it says in verse 16, "In place of your fathers will be your sons; you shall make them princes in all the earth." I see in this passage the influence of a mother. She had the responsibility of making them *princes* in all the earth. She could so train them that they would one day be in positions of authority. What a privilege!

Thank You for Letting Me Be Your Mother

On Mother's Day seven years ago all of my children were home. Only my oldest son was married at the time, and we had only one grandchild. I decided to write each of them a little note to thank them for letting me be their mother. After lunch all of the family gathered in the family room, and I read each note to each child and then one to my husband. They were never intended to be read by anyone else, but to let you know what a privilege I count it to be a mother, I have included these "love notes" by permission of each of them.

For Stephen

I was only twenty-one
    when you came
        into my life.
Much too young to know
    what mothering
        was all about.
But you taught me
    and I loved it.

You were curious and
    an excellent student;

You loved numbers
and Lincoln Logs.

You were all boy!
You loved to run and
play ball;
But still you had
a gentle side.

A song was in your soul
When you were just
a little boy.

Today you are a man,
with wife and baby
of your own.
Instead of nursery rhymes
and building blocks
for you,
You have Renae to play
and sing with.
You're building a
home of your own.

You've shared your
song with me;
You're producing music
to bless others
for the Lord.

Stephen: Your name means "crowned one."
You have caused us to rejoice!

May you be a crown to
your Savior—
"Crowned with glory and honor."

I only pray that your keen mind
be used to reason for your Lord;
That your song be sung for Him;

That you desire to know Him who
truly knows you.

Thank you for letting me be your Mother!

To Gayle

A little girl with big brown eyes,
you came into my life
And wrapped your arms around my neck
and your love around my heart.

You also loved to run and play and
ride high upon the swing.
With trombone in hand you marched
and played your song.

You loved to draw and had quite
an artistic flair;
But where you best excelled was
with your table tennis racket in your hand.

You've grown up to be a beauty;
You think just like your Dad.
You have talents for writing and
for teaching too.

Your quick wit keeps us all
in stitches.
The future lies before you—
May God lead you in the
days ahead.

You are my prophetess
with keen insight from the Lord.

Gayle: Your name means "source of joy."

May your logical mind and quick
wit be used to bring life and
joy to those around you.

May your able tongue be given
over to teaching the Word of God,
and counseling those who are
wandering and confused.

Thank you for letting me be your Mother!

For David

With great anticipation I waited
for your birth;
It was the first time I had a
little nursery.
You were a quiet child,
but I discovered although you
weren't always talking,
You were always listening
and learning.

With your keen mind
you studied maps and
zip code books.
You loved to read anything
from the Bible to encyclopedias.

When you were just seven
you read the Bible through.
You learned the books of the Bible
forward—then backward.

When you were eleven God spoke to you
about being a missionary
But that was laid aside for other
ambitions, until God spoke His "word"
again to you at camp a few years back.

You took piano when a little boy,
then laid *it* aside;

But God wouldn't let you forget the song
  He placed within your heart.
So in these past few years the music and
  the message flow as your heart
    sings unto God.

That missions call can be heard loud
  and clear as even now you prepare
    to go to speak His word around the world.

David: Your name means "beloved."

You are beloved by us and God;
You are chosen to share His Word.
God holds the secret as to how and where.
Be obedient to every command
He will do the rest!

  Thank you for letting me be your Mother!

To Janice

Last, but not least,
  you came into my life
    a month early;
And now you are an early riser.

You loved to sing and play and draw
  bright and happy and unusual things.
    (Remember the snorks!)

You've been quite a student;
  You wanted to please,
    and pleasing you are.

You are a "dreamer," a "romantic,"
  You love to search the Scriptures
    for symbolic meanings,
  You love to praise, even when
    things go wrong.

Music flows through your
fingers and your voice.

Janice: Your name means "gracious gift,"
and indeed you are to me.
May your love for people
provide many opportunities
to share the love of Jesus.

May your love for music be
used to praise His holy name.
May your keen mind and ability
to write be used to communicate
salvation's plan.

Thank you for letting me be your Mother!

To Philip

You were my little son, whom God used
so much in my life.
You were a beautiful baby;
You were loved by us all.
You had added so much to our lives,
But God had a special plan for you.

He had a special home where He
wanted you to live.
When He called, "Philip,"
You answered, "Yes, Lord!"

He's invited us all to come and
live with you and Jesus.
He's preparing a huge mansion
for all of us there.

You were with me only a
few brief months,
But you taught me the greatest

lesson I've ever learned—
to totally depend
on Jesus.

I didn't understand it then;
I know I will one day.
But I've been able to comfort many
who were sad, dear Philip—
all because of you.

Thank you for letting me be your Mother!

(Today, May 11th, 1980 makes twenty-two
years since Philip died)

To Adrian

You, who first dropped love notes by my desk;
Who walked me home from school;
Who first held my hand;
And promised to love 'til death do us part.

First it was one baby
Then two and
three
Then four and
five.

You've loved me and you've
loved each child.
You were my lover, my husband,
Then a father to my "brood."

Adrian: Your names means "creative one."

I pray God will continue
to use your life;
to create love and
unity and faith.

Thank you for letting me be a Mother!

I cannot begin to tell you what a privilege it is to be a mother! And I cannot begin to tell you what a lie of Satan's it is that children are a curse, so much that this generation murders them in the womb. It is Satan's lie that they prevent us from finding career fulfillment. Indeed they are the means God has provided for our fulfillment. It is Satan's lie that they keep us from affording the luxuries of this world. Indeed they are the greatest of earthly treasures—the treasure that we can take with us to heaven. Oh, I didn't say they weren't hard work, that they didn't involve sacrifice, and tears, and plenty of the mundane. But *nothing, absolutely nothing* is gained in this life without hard work and sacrifice.

Not Totally Responsible

As parents, you and I have a tremendous responsibility to train our children. But we must realize that each child has a will of his own. Even if he has been raised in a godly manner, he can choose wrong. Adam and Eve lived in a perfect environment with God, their *Heavenly* Father, as their Teacher. *They* chose to sin. Did *God* fail? ". . . though I taught them, rising up early and teaching them, yet they have not hearkened to receive instruction" (Jer. 32:33). You and I might be partly to blame for our children's failures because we did not train them correctly. But we may *not* be to blame. They may have chosen against what they knew was right. We, as parents, do have a heavy responsibility but not the *total* responsibility. They have the responsibility to choose to practice that which they have been taught.

MARY, THE MODEL MOTHER

We have already seen what an example Mary was in submission to God's word in relation to the virgin birth. I also believe that she was the *model mother*.

She Rocked the Cradle

She rocked the cradle of the
  One Who ruled the world
Held Him in her arms
  Watched Him grow
    from day to day.

She was the one who taught
  Him how to read
    to make His bed
    pick up His toys,
      kneel down to pray.

He was subject unto her
  Until the time appointed
And then she let Him go—
  He then took control

Became the Master
  of the wind and sea
Conquered death and hell
Became my Lord
  and *hers*.

This woman who rocked
  the cradle of the
    One Who ruled
      the world.

—JR

The Obedience of Mary

The first quality we observe in Mary as the mother of Jesus is her *obedience*. The angel had told her before Jesus was conceived in her womb that she was to name her baby Jesus. She obeyed this command. Also she obeyed the command for her baby to be circumcised on the eighth day.

> And when eight days were accomplished for the circumcising of the child, His name was called Jesus, which was so named of the angel before He was conceived in the womb (Matt. 1:21).

The law of Moses had a commandment in reference to Mary's purification. She obeyed this command.

> . . . when the days of her purification according to the law of Moses were accomplished, they brought him to Jerusalem, to present Him to the Lord; as it is written in the law of the Lord, Every male that openeth the womb shall be called holy to the Lord (Matt. 1:22).

There was a special law that pertained to the presentation of Jesus to the Lord. A sacrifice was to be made in His behalf. She obeyed this law.

> . . . to offer a sacrifice according to that which is said in the law of the Lord, a pair of turtledoves, or two young pigeons (Matt. 1:24).

> . . . when the parents brought in the child Jesus, to do for Him after the custom of the law (Matt. 1:27).

Blessing Follows Obedience

Blessing always follows obedience. As Mary was in the process of obeying the law as it pertained to her new baby boy, a just and devout man named Simeon was led by the Spirit into the Temple. He took the baby Jesus up in his arms and, first of all, blessed God, for it had been "revealed unto him by the Holy Spirit that he should not see death, before he had seen the Lord's Christ" (Luke 2:26).

Then "Simeon blessed them, and said unto Mary His mother, Behold, this child is set for the fall and rising again of many in Israel, and for a sign which shall be spoken against; Yea, a sword shall pierce through thy own soul also, that the thoughts of many hearts may be revealed" (Luke 2:34-35).

Each child given to us is a miracle from God, though not in the same way as was Mary's miracle child. We, too, should make our presentation of that gift back to God. I have done that with each of my children. Mary indeed received multiplied blessings as she had the privilege of mothering Jesus in a unique way.

I have received untold blessings in the process of raising my children. I have had the blessing of seeing each of them trust Christ as their own personal Savior and be baptized. I have seen God use each child's unique personality and gifts to be a blessing to others. I cannot describe to you the blessing it has been to hear one sing a song he or she wrote, to play the piano and the guitar as instruments of praise to our God, to give wise counsel, to take charge in a crisis, to teach the Word of God, to lead the music, to edit and type books and messages, to teach their own child to sing and memorize Scripture, to see their talents exhibited in the decorating of their homes, to witness the love and patience exhibited in the disciplining and training of their children.

Mary's blessing also contained "a sword of sorrow," for she knew that her Son one day would be given up to suffer and die for the sins of the whole world. Even so, every mother's blessing contains "a sword" in her soul. For with motherhood invariably comes heartache. When your child suffers heartbreak, you will too. It will be a double grief because of your love for him or her.

John's Gospel tells us that ". . . there stood by the cross of Jesus His mother." Let's stand with Mary at the cross. Can any of us imagine what she felt? I think not. But let us try! Imagine what you would feel if He were your son—and He had done no wrong. Yes, how apt the words of Simeon, "Yea, a sword shall pierce through thy own soul also, that the thoughts of many hearts may be revealed" (Luke 2:34).

Just recently my husband and I rode from the airport with a worn-looking taxi-driver, who had a son in prison. She said she didn't go to church because for twelve years she had visited her son in prison on Sundays.

Yes, she was a mother with a "sword in her heart." Before we left we paused and prayed with her for her and her son. "Oh God, please send someone to water the seed that was planted. Heal her broken heart and save her and her wayward son."

The Parenting of Mary

Her Concern

Every godly mother has a true concern for her child. We see Mary's concern revealed when she lost Jesus in the Temple when He was twelve years old. Supposing He was among the other travelers, Mary and Joseph went a whole day's journey before they realized that Jesus was missing. After three days they found Him in the Temple talking to the doctors of the Law. Although they were amazed, His mother's *concern* was evident: ". . . and His mother said unto Him, Son, why hast Thou thus dealt with us? behold, Thy father and I have sought Thee sorrowing" (Luke 2:48).

Jesus replied, "How is it that ye sought me? Wist ye not that I must be about my Father's business?" (Luke 2:49). His parents didn't understand His comment. Mary stored this in her "computer." "His mother kept all these things and pondered them in her heart" (Luke 2:19).

Mary didn't understand many things in regard to her Son right away and neither will we understand many things regarding *our* children. But we should follow Mary's example as we ponder many circumstances in our hearts.

Mary's Control

The Bible tells us that after the incident in the Temple Jesus "went down with them, and came to Nazareth, and was subject unto them" (Luke 2:51). Mary *took control* over the things that were rightfully hers. She left to God the things that were rightfully His. She refused to "play God," but she couldn't refuse to be a mother. The art of motherhood is to know the difference. You and I must do a lot of *pondering*. It didn't come easy to Mary, and it won't come easy for you and me. There should be *less pronouncing* and *more pondering*. That means at times we must almost bite our tongues in half. You can't be a good mother without some "scars on your tongue." So *proper parenting* God's way is to *ponder and pray*.

It's not our job to have a will *for* our child but to be an avenue to help them discover *God's* will. When Mary said, "Be it unto me according to your word" (Luke 1:38), it didn't just mean the *conception of a child* but also the *completion of the child*.

Relinquishing Control

Mary, along with Joseph, was put in charge of Jesus' oversight, and He was subject to them. Every child must be under the authority of his parents to receive God's protection and blessings. But the day comes when we as mothers must finally relinquish this control. It's done most effectively a little at a time from the period they are very young until the day they move out of your house. Some points of releasing control are more dramatic than others. There is a progression of events that point to this release:

1. Leaving with a baby sitter
2. Playing at someone else's house
3. Spending the night with a friend
4. Going to school
5. Going to camp

6. Going on the first date
7. Going to college
8. Getting married

For some mothers sending their "baby" off to first grade is traumatic. For others it is pure relief. Off to college is definitely a crisis point, as is marriage. A child's moving out of town is a real heartbreaker (take it from me, I've been through it with all four of my children).

Someone has called this process "cutting the apron strings." You'll always be their mother, but your responsibilities are changing. You're working to the place where:

> You may consult
> but not control
> You may counsel
> but not coerce
> You may bless
> but not boss.

I believe that a "crisis point" for Mary was at the wedding at Cana. Mary was probably a good planner. She noticed when the refreshments ran out. She went and told Jesus, "They have no wine" (John 2:3). Jesus saith unto her, "Woman, what have I to do with thee?" I think what Jesus was saying was, "Mother, you must stop telling Me what to do." She then told the servants, "Whatsoever He saith unto you, do it" (John 2:5). Or, in other words, "*He's* in charge."

I believe that Mary had this revelation, "You should stop giving orders and start taking them." It's unthinkable that what she told them to do she was unwilling to do. This was some of the best advice ever given:

The Source—"Whatever *He* says . . ."
The Scope—"*Whatever* He says . . ."
The Service—"Whatever He says, *do it.*"

The story in Matthew 12:46-50 has always caused a pang in my heart for Mary, Jesus' mother. I guess I felt *for* her what *I* would have felt. Remember that was the occasion when Jesus' mother and brothers were waiting outside to speak with Him. But Jesus replied, "Who is my mother? and who are my brethren? And He stretched forth His hand toward His disciples, and said, Behold my mother and my brethren. For whosoever shall do the will of my Father which is in heaven, the same is my brother, and sister, and mother."

You see, Mary's relationship was unique to all other mother-son relationships, but there is *some* similarity. Yes, He was her son in the flesh, but He was her Savior spiritually. And spiritually she had no greater place than any other person. She must acknowledge, "My Son— *the* Savior." But she must also confess, "My Son, *my* Savior." He wanted her to recognize the difference. She must not only relinquish control as a mother, but she must recognize His spiritual authority over her.

We must relinquish control and acknowledge:

> My son—the minister of music
> My daughter—the minister's wife
> My son—the missionary
> My daughter—the mother

We should affirm our grownup children in their roles and treat them with respect. We are training them to take spiritual leadership roles as well as to be mature adults.

When this final day has come, what a joy and freedom it is if you have done a good job. Anna Mow said that you've succeeded as a parent when you've worked yourself out of a job, but not out of a relationship. You will never want the *responsibilities* of motherhood again. I have never once missed carpool. I never remember missing changing diapers or wiping runny noses. I've never missed refereeing disagreements or reminding my children to clean up their rooms.

But I have sorely missed the fellowship of my grownup children when they were far away. How thankful I am for the telephone and for the mail service. Last Mother's Day was complete when the last child called to say "I love you." I still think up thoughtful surprises for birthdays and Christmas. I still "mother" my children.

My David was overseas for two Christmases. Mothers get extra sentimental when their children are not home for Christmas. Monetarily, it's not really worth sending gifts overseas by air mail, and it could take two or three months to mail by boat. He was on a ship that sailed from port to port, so a gift by boat might not catch up with him. We decided just to write that we had deposited some money in his savings account.

But to a mother that's not enough. So I had this idea— to pack a shoe box with symbols of Christmas and send it air mail. I had so much fun Christmas shopping for this twenty-five-year-old son—buying fun things to remind him of Christmas and family. The box contained a Snoopy Christmas stocking, a stuffed Smurf, a Christmas card that played carols, an expandable Christmas greeting that stretched to about four feet and said, "Merry Christmas!" a Christmas candle, an artificial poinsettia bloom, and some homemade cookies (they arrived all crumbled, but he ate them anyway). I knew this "boy" was a man, but I wanted to "mother" him at Christmas.

While Mary no longer "managed" Jesus, she still "mothered" Him. She stood at the foot of His Cross and wept. And though she did not outrank you and me spiritually, Jesus cared for her as a mother right up until the end. On the Cross He appointed John to watch over her when He was gone. "Behold your mother! Behold your son!" (John 19:26-27).

After They're Grown, What?

The Influence of Prayer

One important influence that will not end even after your children are grown and out from under your control is the *influence of prayer*. Someone has said that at this period of a child's life a parent's motto should be,

> Hands off, prayers on
> Mouths shut, hearts open.

I remember when our oldest son was first married that one Sunday night we came home, and he and his wife had not gone to church, but were at our house watching television. I felt like marching in and declaring, "If you don't go to church, you can't watch my television." I'm so glad I didn't do that. I decided instead to bite my tongue.

We didn't have a problem with our relationship, so why should I create one? I decided instead to pray.

On their wedding day, I had claimed for them the promises in Psalm 84. I began to intensify my prayer for them in verse 4, "Blessed are they that dwell in Thy house: they will be still praising Thee." Today my son is a minister of music, praising and serving the Lord.

I've had the privilege of praying for my children's mates *before* they were married. I also have the privilege of praying about *their* concerns *after* marriage. I have prayed more hours during their transitional times and new opportunities in vocational guidance. It's so much better to pray than to worry. I've had the privilege of praying for my children in their times of grief and trouble. The tears flowed as I prayed through loss, through miscarriage, broken relationships and disappointments.

Oh, there is also the joy of *answered* prayer. I've held little baby Michael in my arms—an answer to prayer for Gayle and Mike in which I had a vital part.

Then there's my most recent answer to prayer in behalf of a child.

Several years ago when David left to go overseas the Lord gave me a paraphrase of Proverbs 31 which I presented to David. He said that I could share it with you.

A Paraphrase of Proverbs 31

The words of David's mother which she taught him:

What, my son?
   The son for whom I
prayed

Whom God miraculously
saved that he should be
"beloved" in His sight
and a joy to his mother's heart.
The son for whom I
prepared
and gave to the Lord before
and after he was born.
The son from whom I
pondered what *purpose* God had
for him.
The son whom God called to
leave his father and mother
to go to the ends of the earth
to tell the good news of
His blessed Son.

It is not for God's servants,
O David
It is not for God's servants
to hold earthly relationships
too dear—
Nothing or no one should *ever*
come first in your life;
God must be preeminent.

For you must pray for those
who don't know God
For those who will die
without a Savior.

You must tell the lost how
Jesus loves them and
died for them.
You must plead with those
who are physically

and spiritually hungry
to come to Him who is
the "Bread of Life."

* * * * * * * * * * * * *

I long for you to find a
virtuous wife
For her price will be
far above rubies.
Your heart will trust her
You will lack nothing
for she will satisfy
your needs
as long as you live.

She will be a willing worker
She'll know proper nutrition
and plan balanced meals;
She'll be a wise shopper
and won't waste money.

She will share your concern
for the needy and
want to open her
heart and home
to those who need
the Lord.

She'll be a gracious hostess
and make people
from all walks of life
feel at ease.
She will know how to buy
clothes wisely
She will have good taste
and dress modestly
and appropriately.

For she should conduct herself
in a way becoming to
the wife of a
Christian leader.

She should be industrious
and creatively use
her talents
in the service of
the Lord.
She will be a mature Christian
and be well spoken of
for her fine reputation.

* * * * * * * * * * * * *

She'll know the wise things
to say
She won't gossip or say the
first thing that comes
to her mind.
She will have a gentle
and quiet spirit;
She'll know how to organize
her work and won't
waste her time.

She'll love children and
they will love her and
be glad she is their
mother.

You will be greatly blessed
and will praise *her*.
You will be proud that this
lovely woman is
your wife

She will not just be charming
   and beautiful,
      for these will fade
But she will have a deep love
   and reverence
      for God.

She will love God's Word and
   be a woman of prayer.
Everyone will recognize that
   she is a godly woman
      because of what she
         says and does.
She will be committed to going
   wherever God leads you
      and will be content with
         whatever God provides.
                                —JR

When David returned from two years as a volunteer missionary, it was so good to see him and to be able to reach out and touch him, but I longed that he might meet that helper God had chosen for him. I knew that mother-love only went so far. I've prayed all of his life for that "special" girl whom God would send, but I intensified my prayers for her.

I didn't ask for someone short or tall, with blue eyes or brown, alto or soprano. I didn't request that she could sing or play the piano, that she be rich or pretty. The "girl of my prayers" was a Proverbs 31 girl—one who loved God and who would love my David, someone who would think he was "Mr. Wonderful," who would build him up, encourage and challenge him as he sought to serve the Lord, and who wanted to be a homemaker and have a family.

Oh, God has more than answered my prayers. Kelly is the "girl of my prayers." She's all this and more. She's beautiful inside and out. She loves God and wants to serve Him above all. But her eyes light up when David comes in the room and my David has a "glow" when she's around.

How I praise God for the far-reaching and continual influence of prayer!

Part II

Spheres of Influence – Yielded to the Lordship of Christ

God Is In Control

The Psalmist said, "Thou hast put all things under His feet" (Ps. 8:6). God indeed established a *line of authority,* and *He* is the main authority over all things. This is not an oppressive thought but the most comforting concept in my life—*God is in control.* Another way of putting it is *He is over all* and *He is in charge.*

Some years ago we experienced an earth tremor in Memphis, Tennessee. I will never forget it. I was sitting in church when the chandelier overhead began to sway slightly. One person, then another, began slowly to get up before anyone really grasped what was happening. I finally reached my family, and we were grateful that by that time the tremor was over. On the way home my youngest daughter, Janice, asked, "Mama, what do you do when there is an earthquake?" Besides a few practical suggestions, I answered, "Remember, Janice, *God* is in control." Yes, He is sovereign! *He* is *over* all.

That evening when we arrived home I got my Bible and reread a passage of Scripture I had read in my morning devotions that had puzzled me. Psalm 18:10 said, "And He rode upon a cherub and did fly: yes, He did fly upon the wings of the wind." God was symbolically pictured as flying upon a cherub. As I meditated on this verse in the light of the evening's happenings, I concluded that this verse was saying, God is in control, and He is not in a panic. He sees the storms, the earthquakes of life, and they are *under* His feet. The psalmist tells us in verse sixteen, "He sent from above, He took me, He drew me out of many waters."

I can put my confidence in a God who is in control not only of the literal floods and earthquakes, but also the tremors in my life. I can also trust Him that at His appointed time He will rescue me so the circumstances of life will be *under my* feet.

God's Line of Authority

Though equality exists in the Godhead, there is a spiritual line of authority. God the Father is the head of God the Son (1 Cor. 11:3). This does not indicate inferiority. God the Father has chosen to give His Son the highest place of honor. "*Every* knee shall bow and *every* tongue confess that Jesus Christ is Lord to the glory of God the Father" (Phil. 2:10-11).

God has committed all judgment to the Son. This Son, who humbled himself and willingly left heaven to die in our place, has been given by His Father a name which is above every name (Phil. 2:9). But 1 Corinthians 15:27-28 declares,

> And when all things shall be subdued unto Him, then shall the Son also Himself be subject unto Him that put all things *under* Him, that God may be all in all.

It is made clear that the Father is *excepted* Who put all things under the Son. There was no jealousy in the Godhead—no striving for first place. For there was no inferiority, only different positions. Jesus had been appointed such a place of honor that there was no coveting of position. After all it was Jesus who not only was *sent* by the Father to be a servant and to die, but it was Jesus who willingly *gave* His life for us. They were in such complete oneness that thoughts of competition never occurred.

"I Was Sent"

I was *sent*
  by My Father
    into the world.

I must work His works!

I didn't come to do My will
  He *sent* Me to do His will;
I didn't come to speak My words
  He *sent* Me to speak what
    I heard Him say.

My Father told Me
  to tell you
    to believe in Me
      to love Me
        to honor Me.
If you don't honor Me
  You don't honor my Father
    Who *sent* Me.

If you believe in Me
  My Father will give you
    everlasting life;

I will raise you up at
the last day.

You can have that life
right now—
The living Father sent Me
And I live by the Father;
If I am your bread you
shall live by Me.
True life will begin today
and you shall live
forever.

So, you want to see
my Father!
If you've seen Me,
you've seen Him
who *sent* Me.

I and my Father are one and
I always do those things
that please Him.
Soon I'm going back
to my Father—
to Him that *sent* Me.
That's really best for you
because when I go
I'm going to *send* another—
the Comforter
My Spirit!

He'll not only be with you
as I have been;
He'll be *in* you
He'll never leave you;
He'll glorify Me
He'll show you all things.

Then you'll really know Me—
  The One the Father *sent*.
Then I'll be in you as the
  Father is in Me.
And as the Father has *sent* Me
  even so will I *send* you

That others too may know
  that *I was sent*.

—JR

It is difficult for us human beings to comprehend someone being *over* another without mixing feelings of superiority or someone being *under* another without feelings of
inferiority. But God demonstrated in His very person the
concepts of true equality of worth, oneness, and at the
same time a line of authority.

It was not offensive to God the Son that God the
Father was His head (1 Cor. 11:3c). He never rebelled
that His Father sent Him to be the Savior of the world
(John 17:18). He never complained that He only got to
do what His Father told Him to do and that He only got
to say what His Father told Him to say (see John 8:28-
29).

Hebrews 6:8-9 says, "Though He were a son, yet
learned He obedience by the things which He suffered;
and being made perfect, He became the author of eternal salvation unto all them that obey Him." For when
Jesus, the Son, was *under* the authority of His Father,
He was then given the authority *over* heaven and earth
(Matt. 28:18).

If we can only see what God has in store for *us*, what

authority He wants to give *us* if we can only learn to live *under* authority. He said, "Blessed are the meek [the submissive] for they shall inherit the earth" (Matt. 5:5). We can have all things under *our* feet if we are *in Christ*—living in submission to Him and to those to whom He has delegated authority.

Delegated Authority

God is the undisputed One in charge of this universe. It would have been no problem for Him to have a corner on all authority and not to share it with anyone. He could have spoken His commands and wishes audibly for all to hear. At a certain time each day He could have all human beings stand at attention to get their daily instructions from their Authority. He could have ruled the universe any way He chose. How marvelous that He chose to share His authority with us. God set up specific spheres of influence for our lives and delegated His authority in these areas. He has done this for our protection.

Under God's Protection

How excellent is Thy lovingkindness, O God! therefore the children of men put their trust under the shadow of Thy wings (Psalm 36:7).

The Bible symbolizes God's protection in various ways. One of my favorites is "under His wings." So when I yield to His authority in my life I reap the benefits of living "under His wings." The hymnwriter, William O. Cushing, has beautifully expressed this thought.

Under His wings I am safely abiding,
Tho the night deepens and tempests are
   wild;
Still I can trust Him, I know He will keep
   me,
He has redeemed me and I am His child.

Under His wings, what a refuge in sorrow!
How the heart yearningly turns to His rest!
Often when earth has no balm for my
   healing,
There I find comfort and there I am blest.

Under His wings, O what precious
   enjoyment!
There will I hide till life's trials are o'er:
Sheltered, protected, no evil can harm me,
Resting in Jesus I'm safe evermore.

Under His wings, under His wings,
Who from His love can sever?
Under His wings my soul shall abide,
Safely abide forever.

In every area of our lives God has delegated various authorities for our protection. He's saying, "I love you; don't hurt yourself." We sometimes chafe under this supposed bondage, thinking how wonderful it would be if we could only be free of those over us.

Just suppose that there were no speed limit in a school zone. Many of us might run over a careless child. If there were no parents to tell a child what time to go to bed and what nutritious foods to eat, children would be unhealthy and die at an early age. If there were no pastors to warn of false doctrines, many would be led astray and spend a Christless eternity.

Jesus wept over Jerusalem. He wanted to gather her children together, even as a hen gathereth her chickens *under her wings* (Matt. 23:37). He longed to protect His people, but they refused. Truly, to come *under* His delegated authority is to be covered by His protection.

There are three major spheres of our lives where God has delegated authority.

Headship in the Home

The very first sphere of influence where we encounter authority is in the home. The home was instituted by God in the Garden of Eden and takes precedence in its importance and influence over all other areas of life.

God had an orderly plan for the home. He saw the need for a leader—someone in charge. He placed the man at the head of the home.

> But I would have you know that the head of every man is Christ; and the head of the woman is the man; and the head of Christ is God (1 Cor. 11:3).

> Wives, submit yourselves unto your own husbands, as unto the Lord. For the husband is the head of the wife, even as Christ is the head of the church: and He is the Saviour of the body (Eph. 5:22-23).

This position was in no wise a put down on the woman to show that she was inferior. In the same verse God demonstrates the submission of Christ to God the Father, and we have already seen that this was not demeaning to Christ. No, position has nothing to do with these feelings of superiority versus inferiority. Sin has caused the abuses and misuses of our God-given positions. We must learn to deal with sin instead of always trying to change our roles. If we *do* change our roles and sin continues, it will only result in worse heartache.

So we see that the man is God's appointed leader in the home. Then we discover that the woman also has authority in the home. She is *over* her children along with her husband and *under* his leadership. Ephesians 6:1 says, "Children, obey your parents." She is also *over* the management of the home. She is to be a "keeper at home"—to guide or rule the affairs of her home (Titus 2:5).

In summary, God has delegated His authority in the home to the father *and* the mother. But Dad has the final word—he is the head. This does not mean that the man should rule excessively or selfishly. No, that would be an *abuse* and is sometimes caricatured as a norm for those who believe in male headship. Nothing is farther from the truth. The man who leads with a servant spirit wins the loving followship of his family.

God's Governmental Ministers

When society grew to a certain stage, God delegated some of His authority to human government. Romans 13:1 says, "For there is no power but of God: the powers that be are ordained of God." God saw that to keep order in society as we related to each other, there had to be some guidelines and someone, an authority, to enforce them. Romans 13:4 states that the one whom God puts in charge of keeping order in society is a "minister of God, a revenger to execute wrath on him that doeth evil."

We are charged to be subject to the higher powers or rulers. In verse 6 we are also told to pay our taxes so government might be able to function efficiently. We are utterly to forsake personal revenge and to turn our vengeance for wrongs over to God's governmental ministers. It is God who has placed those in charge of society that we might live "quiet and peaceable lives" (1 Tim. 2:2).

We see many abuses in government today, but we could not be so foolish as to abolish the authority of government because of the personal abuses of some. Indeed we must work to correct abuses.

There are different types of human government. A few of them are as follows:

A REPUBLIC—a government in which supreme power resides in a body of citizens entitled to vote and is exercised by elected officers and representatives responsible to them and governing according to law

A MONARCHY—a government which has undivided rule or absolute sovereignty by a single person

An OLIGARCHY—a government in which a small group exercises control, especially for corrupt and selfish purposes

A DICTATORSHIP—a form of government in which absolute power, often oppressive or contemptuously overbearing toward others, is concentrated in a dictator or a small clique

COMMUNISM—a totalitarian system of government in which a single authoritarian party controls state-owned means of production with the professed aim of establishing a classless society

We could debate the worth of each type of government and its economic system. This lies outside the purpose of this book, but the bottom line is whether those in charge are godly or wicked.

We in the United States look with disdain upon a dictatorship. We see it as oppressive. There is certainly a tendency to oppression with those who have total power. But there is also the danger of the misuse of a democracy. If the people are wicked, they will elect wicked leaders. They will pass wicked laws and judge unjustly. This type of government can also be unbearable. There must be godly rulers, or all human government will be a failure. God's Word says, "When the righteous are in authority, the people rejoice; but when the wicked bear rule, the people mourn" (Ps. 29:2).

Since I live in a country that is a republic, I am allowed a voice in my government. It is my responsibility to help right the wrongs. Yes, this is *my* country and through it I can make it a better place.

My Country

My country right or wrong?
Certainly not!
But indeed, my country.
My country
to love

to pray for
to work for.

Other countries I love to visit
to marvel at their beauty
to be astounded at their past
to wish them a blessing
for their future.

But this is my country
the land of my birth
the land of my family
the land of my freedom
and opportunity.

Other families are of great worth
But one family claims
my highest devotion and love;
Other lands and people have qualities
I admire
But one land
one country
claims my greatest
loyalty and respect.

I know best the weaknesses
of my family members
and yet I love them—
Long to help them
to pray
to strengthen them
Because God uniquely
gave them to me.

Yes, I know the weaknesses
of my country
But I will pray
I will be involved

to help change
　　to right the wrongs;
Because God chose my country
　　to be the place where
　　　　I was born
　　to be the place where
　　　　my influence
　　　　　　could be felt.

I love all the peoples
　　of the world
Because "God so loved the world."
Yet God had a plan
　　to set apart
　　　　uniquely different people in
　　　　　　uniquely different countries
　　　　　　　　with different foods and
　　　　　　　　　　different customs
　　　　　　　　　　　　different speech and
　　　　　　　　　　　　different looks.

This was God's idea
　　not ours—
He must have a reason
　　a purpose for mankind
And even though He loved the world,
He chose one nation
　　one people and
　　　　one Land
　　to be uniquely His;
He had a special purpose
　　a special love for them.

I do not live in that country
　　and yet to me
　　　　it's special!

I love to visit His Land
I love its mountains
   I love its valleys
     I love its brooks
     and streams.

I love the people who
   live in that Land;
They're called His people—
   His *chosen* people
They have a special love
   for their Land
     a patriotism
       a pride in their country.
This country called Israel.

I am inspired by their
   love for their Land;
My visits to their country
   have blessed my life—
     have challenged me.

I long that the people of
   that Land may know
     my Savior
And I have a special love
   for those who do know
     and love my Lord.

My heart is stirred as I
   visit other lands;
At the oneness that I
   feel with these vastly
     different peoples.
I know that in a sense,
   in Christ
I have a bond with them that

transcends all others
my family and
my country,
Because they are part of
the body of Christ.

But though we are one on
this earth,
we *are* different
and God planned it so;
different countries with
different peoples
are God's idea
not mine.

God has another plan
for another time;
In a country called heaven
in the sweet bye and bye;
Where all the saved will
live together
Where we'll know as we
are known
Where God Himself will rule
Where the peoples of all the
earth will gather
'round His throne.

But until then, I'll be
living out His plan
for now;
Working with the people
of my country
to make this world
a better place
a peaceful place

And sharing with them
that peace will only come
to our country
to all countries
through Jesus Christ
God's chosen Prince of Peace!

—JR

Spiritual Authority in The Church

Jesus said, "I will build my church" (Matt. 16:18). The New Testament pattern clearly shows that *spiritual authority* was given to the church. God's plan of delegated authority for the church is that under Christ pastors or elders are "in charge." They watch for your soul. The pastor's authority should not be self-conscious lording it over others. He should have a servant spirit as his own Lord did. This was best illustrated when Jesus took a towel and washed His disciples' feet. But nonetheless he will communicate a God-given authority that others recognize and follow. He is the undershepherd, Jesus being the Chief Shepherd over him.

> Remember them which have the rule over you, who have spoken unto the word of God: whose faith follow, considering the end of their conversation (Heb. 13:7).
>
> Obey them that have the rule over you for they watch for your souls (Heb. 13:17).

Certainly there have been abuses to the role of pastor. The Ghana tragedy some years ago, when Jim Jones led one thousand followers to the supposed "promised land," only to commit mass suicide, is sufficient warning to the gullible. God has established checks and balances. If a pastor is not teaching and living the truth of God's Word, he forfeits his God-given authority.

God has also given deacons to be helpers in the leadership role of the church. The office of deacon is a sacred responsibility with high qualifications (1 Tim. 3:1-10). The pastor must give himself to the main duties of prayer and ministry of the Word (Acts 6:4). He needs the help and counsel of other wise men.

The wives of the pastor and deacons have an important place of helper to their husbands. Their personal and home lives must be equally exemplary (1 Tim. 3:11). There are also some single women who dedicate themselves to be the servants of the church (1 Cor. 7:34; Rom. 16:1-2).

An Orderly System

Everywhere you go you meet authority. You might not recognize it until you need it, but it is there. If it is not, the result is chaotic. You may never see the manager of a restaurant, but if someone makes a disturbance, he will likely make a quick appearance.

You may decide it is a small thing to run a red light or a stop sign, or exceed the speed limit. But if you cause an accident, soon the lights will be flashing and sirens blaring, and "authority" will appear.

A child may constantly be a behavior problem, causing a disturbance in the classroom, disrupting the learning process. This, however, cannot be allowed. The teacher will exercise her authority through correction or low conduct grades. If this doesn't suffice, the child can be taken to a higher authority, the principal's or counselor's office.

How I praise God for a system of orderly authority. It is built into every area of life—home, government, church, business, school, and even miscellaneous. God has planned it this way. He means it for our protection and good. He has chosen to involve *us* in His governing process. He delegated His authority in different spheres of life to different people.

Who's in Charge, Anyway?

How do you get to be "in charge"? How are you chosen for one of God's delegated leadership positions? It is so simple that most people miss it. You're in training right now. In fact, you've been in training all of your life. You learn how to be "in charge" by learning how to be *obedient.* As someone has well put it, "You can't be *over* unless you're *under.*"

When you were in grammar school and the teacher would leave the room for a short time, she would leave someone "in charge," to be a monitor. Did she choose the class rowdy? No, she chose someone who obeyed the rules. So, God is looking for someone who delights in obeying the rules. He's not looking for someone who simply wants to boss others around.

The Way Up Is Down

In the spiritual realm the way *up* is *down*. The way to rule is by being a *servant*. If God wants to place you somewhere in a larger sphere of influence that's His business. Your job is to be obedient and contented where you are right now. Do you remember Joseph, who was sold into slavery by his brothers? They meant it for harm, but God meant it for good. Joseph was a faithful servant. In God's timing he was promoted to a high place of honor and influence (Gen. 45:4-5). This principle is taught throughout Scripture. Peter puts it like this, "Humble yourselves under the mighty hand of God that He may exalt you in due time" (1 Pet. 5:6).

God's Word says that I am to be a *servant!* No, I *can't* do my own self-centered thing. I am a *de*pendent, not an *in*dependent person. I must glorify God by obeying Him and serving my fellowman. I am born again to be a *servant,* doing *His* thing. It doesn't make me a weakling to recognize that "without *Him* I can do nothing" (John 15:5), but that "I can do *all* things through Christ who strengthens me" (Phil. 4:13).

I'm not exempt from dealing with the heartbreaking problems and the unmerciful storms which are breaking up homes and wrecking lives. I am a *servant.* You are a *servant.* We are God's *servants!* We should give our lives to relieving human heartbreak, but knowing that "it is not *I* but Christ," pointing men and women, boys and girls to the Word of God.

I've seen the heartbreak that sin can bring. I've counseled teenage alcoholics. I've prayed with a young lady who was on the brink of divorce. I've held someone in my arms as she sobbed out her heartbreak over a husband who had just walked out.

I've also seen the healing that *God* can bring. I've witnessed someone who was heartbroken lean totally on Jesus and His written Word. Yes, I've witnessed a miracle. I've seen a home put back together. I've seen changed lives. I've seen someone go to God's Word and claim promise after promise. I've seen these promises fulfilled. What a blessing to be a part of a miracle! I helped pray. I helped encourage that one to look to Jesus, because frankly I had no help without Him. I want to be an *obedient servant,* looking to Jesus and helping others when the storms of life come.

"For Such a Time As This"

We do not know when God will call upon us to be "in charge." You must be pure and obedient before Him at all times, so when He speaks your name you won't have to look around and ask, "Who, me?"

Queen Esther was a wonderful example of a gracious lady who recognized her queenly position. She knew she wasn't the king, but she indeed knew she was the queen. She also knew her privileges and limitations as the queen. When her Uncle Mordecai asked that piercing question, "How canst thou know but that thou art come to the kingdom for such a time as this?" she had to stop and seriously consider the right answer. The whole Jewish nation was in danger of being annihilated.

She *did* had access to the king, the one who was the chief authority. She had been a submissive wife. He loved and admired her greatly, but according to the custom of that day, she couldn't simply tap on the throne room door, peek in, and say, "It's your lover girl just stopping by to ask you a question." No, without an appropriate invitation she could be put to death. But she was *prepared* and she was courageous. There must have been something about the regal way she stood, the care with which she had prepared her appearance, and the attitude which she conveyed that won his heart.

We can only imagine the times she spent alone with God as she yielded her personal rights to her Heavenly King and sought His strength. She fasted and asked others to join her in this God-given assignment. But it wasn't only that day that she prepared herself to gain an audience with the king. It was her daily habit to be beautiful *and* submissive. The king knew her for who she was. With her character established, having prepared herself for the immediate occasion, and being completely dependent on God, she determined to wield her influence. This matter was so strategically important that she was even willing to die. I wonder, will you be prepared like Esther to risk *your* life for *such a time as this?* You've been in training. Will you pass the test?

Biblical Submission

But I would have you know, that the head of every man is Christ; and the head of the woman is the man; and the head of Christ is God (1 Cor. 11:3).

In his outstanding book, *The Christian Family,* Larry Christenson says, "To be submissive means to yield humble and intelligent obedience to an ordained power or authority. The example God gives is that of the Church being submissive to the rule of Christ. Far from being degrading, this is the Church's glory! God did not give this law of wives being submissive to their husbands because He had a grudge against women: on the contrary, He established this order for *the protection of women* and *the harmony of the home.* He means for a woman to be sheltered from many of the encounters of life. Scripture knows nothing of a 50-50 'democratic marriage.' God's order is 100-100. The wife is 100 percent a wife, the husband 100 percent a husband."[1]

I, as a Spirit-filled wife, should willingly *choose* to be submissive to my husband because I know God has ordained this order for my protection and welfare. The husband, of course, carries a great responsibility. He has been appointed by God to be the head of his wife, even as Christ is the head of the Church (Eph. 5:23). He is to love his wife as Christ loved the Church—this will prevent him from being harsh and dictatorial (Eph. 5:25). He should set an example of obedience and submission to God and His Word. If his wife and children see him exceeding the speed limit, hedging on the income-tax, not returning incorrect change, having a disrespectful attitude toward public officials, or not keeping any of God's commandments, he is tearing down his own authority.

A wife should exhibit before her children an example of obedience to God, her husband, and other authorities. If she runs down her husband to her children, not holding him in high esteem, she is undermining not only his, but her own authority. However, if she lives *under authority* God gives her the hearts of her children and she rules with authority.

I remember a time when my then young teenage son, Steve, had done something wrong (I can't even remember what), and I told him to bend over the bed as I administered corporal punishment. I'm still amazed that he did it without resistance. He was stronger than I at the time.

As I look back I think there were probably several reasons. He had been taught to respect his mother. Also, he knew he had done wrong and had been taught that the Bible encouraged discipline. But he also knew that his Daddy's authority stood behind me and that if he wasn't submissive to *my* authority and discipline, he would meet his Daddy's authority when he came home, and it would be even harder.

There was mercy at our house for true, undelayed repentance, but there was sure discipline for several things—for being untruthful, disrespectful, and deliberately disobedient. There was little of these exhibited at our house—for the surety and swiftness of discipline had been demonstrated.

I remember on another occasion we were out driving in the car. David let the window down in the back seat, and his Daddy gently asked, "Son, please put up your window." Well, after a while the window went down again a little bit. Adrian chided, "Son, I told you to put up the window. If you do that one more time, I'm going to punish you." Well, I thought that settled that, but after a few minutes the window went down again, and my husband said quite sternly, "Son!"

I couldn't believe it. I couldn't believe David would so

openly disobey, knowing swift discipline would occur, and I said quite shocked and unbelieving, "David!!!" as if to question, "How could you, Son?" I knew we would stop, and he would be incurring his father's painfully undivided attention, and all so unnecessarily! But to my amazement *and* relief it wasn't David who had let the window down. My husband was playing a trick on me and had quietly touched the automatic switch by his seat that let David's window down. We still laugh about the incident, but we all knew that when Daddy said it, he meant it.

Another instance occurred when our youngest daughter, Janice, was only four. It was her first Sunday in "big church." She got restless and was making some kind of noise. I whispered, "Hush, Janice," and she stopped. But she started the noise again, and I said, "Don't do that." Well, when she did it the third time, I said, "If you do that again I'm going to take you out and spank you."

I thought that would cure her. But not so—she did it again. And so "woman of my word" that I was, I proceeded to pick her up and carry her out as quietly as I could. We were sitting right by the end of the pew, and when I got up she grabbed the end of the pew as hard as she could and started yelling, "Don't spank me! Don't spank me!" Well, that only made it worse. Boy, would she get it now! I was so embarrassed.

I finally pried her fingers off of the pew and was making my way out the back door when my "preacher husband," seeing that everyone was looking anyway, decided to make an object lesson out of this situation and openly acknowledged, "That's *my* daughter, and *my* wife is going to take her out and make her more uncomfortable *outside* than she is *inside*."

Well, I was never more humiliated! (I had to forgive him for that. I wasn't interested in object lessons—I just wanted to get out). Yes, I *did* make it more uncomfortable outside for her. But I was so embarrassed that I didn't come back in. We never had that problem again.

James Dobson's book on *The Strong-Willed Child* came out at the close of my child-rearing days. But I certainly had some. We had some "interesting" times! I agree that the *will*, but not the *spirit* of the child must be broken. On several occasions I thought I would like to break their necks. Oh, but when those "wild horses" are "meeked" what strength and productivity! How I praise God for His help in the process that has yielded such rich benefits. I see my children now struggling with similar strong wills. When their children's little wills are conquered, they will be widely used by God!

When a wife stays under her husband's protective authority, she is shielded physically, emotionally, and *spiritually*. Paul says in 1 Corinthians 11:10, "Therefore she [the wife] should be subject to his [her husband's] authority and should have a covering on her head as a token, a symbol of her submission to authority, because of the angels" (*Amplified Bible*, RSV). Paul recognizes the influence for good a woman who is under the authority of her husband has even on the angels. When Satan rebelled against God, he led a rebellion in heaven among the angels, and his angels were cast out with him (Rev.

12:9). They got out from under God's authority.

When a wife rebels against her husband's authority, she is behaving like Satan and his host of rebels. The angels are observing a woman's submission. The Bible says, "Rebellion is as the sin of witchcraft" (1 Sam. 15:23). When a wife rebels against authority, she opens herself to evil influences—to those fallen angels who still live in rebellion against God and are seeking to oppress, obsess, and possess the lives of human beings.

When a woman lives under her husband's authority, she is protected against satanic forces, and she can have power in prayer, in the exercise of her spiritual gifts, and has authority over Satan and his demons. If we as wives are rebellious, we leave our lives open to Satan. He can use his influence to get in a "tiny crack in our spiritual armor," and build a stronghold of doubt, fear, exaggeration, pride, lust, laziness, and a multitude of other sins.

If we are living *under authority*, we can resist Satan and he will flee (James 4:7). What victory we can know in the spiritual realm!

> In the name of Jesus
> In the name of Jesus
> We have the victory.
> In the name of Jesus
> In the name of Jesus
> Satan will have to flee!

> Who can tell what God can do?
> Who can tell His love for you?
> In the name of Jesus, Jesus
> We have the victory!

"A Helper I Will Be"

When my children were small we sang a little song that
went like this,

> A helper I will be
> A helper I will be
> There's work to do
> There's work to do
> In our family.

God created the first helper. "And the Lord God said,
It is not good that the man should be alone; I will make
him an help meet for him" (Gen. 2:18). God made
Adam *and* Eve to rule, to have dominion over the earth
(Gen. 1:28). Eve was not meant to be a slave, but she
was meant to serve. She was not meant to be a competi-
tor, but a completor! She was the part of Adam that was
missing, and he was thrilled that she was a valuable part
of his team.

God didn't spell out exactly what the woman was to
do, because it would depend on the situation and the
circumstances. But we are told that "the woman was
made for the man and not the man for the woman"
(1 Cor. 11:8). *I* didn't say it, ladies! God did!

A submissive wife has been caricatured as a doormat
type of person—waiting on her husband hand and
foot—always saying, "Yes, dear, yes, dear, that's right,
dear!" Nothing is farther from the truth. A helper isn't just
a "yes person." *The Saturday Evening Post* had a cartoon
which showed an overbearing boss walking down the
hall with an obviously new employee. He was saying,

"Another thing I can't stand, Snively, is a 'yes man.' Do you understand that?"

We would all like someone to admire us and think our ideas are super. But deep inside we also want someone to be honest with us, point out our weaknesses, and challenge us to live on a higher plane. If someone, whether our mate, our best friend, or our associate, always tells us how wonderful we are and never challenges any idea, we are left with an empty feeling. They are either totally uninformed on the subject we are discussing, or they so fear controversy that they cannot express a contrary opinion.

Either way these kinds of people close the door on creativity. There is nothing more challenging to me than to be in a brainstorming session with one or more persons who challenge my creativity, and together we emerge with an idea much better than I could have thought of on my own.

The *secret* of being that valuable associate-consultant is *sensitivity*. First, as a wife you should be secure in your position, knowing it is a God-appointed role, not always competing for first place. That role, of course, is the daily oversight of the household and the children.

With this foundation you are ready to be a counselor. But you must be sensitive to the *time* when your counsel would be best received. This should be a matter of prayer. When your husband is tired or he has other matters of pressing importance to him, it would be a poor time to bring up a subject that is contrary to the direction of his present thought.

My husband doesn't like to discuss "heavy" or controversial subjects in fun or recreational times. It's hard for me not to think of subjects that are important to me at those times. For at last I have his undivided attention—or do I? I have discovered that he will resist some topics of discussion at a time for a pleasant walk or a picnic or a ride in the country. He has another agenda—to clear his mind of business-type matters and to relax. He wants me to enter into *his* present priority. Sometimes a "lighter" subject will suddenly become "heavy," and we as wives should be sensitive enough to know when to "table it" until later.

Queen Esther was a wise woman in this regard. As we have mentioned she had a very serious matter to discuss with the king. Even though she knew she had access to the throne room, she didn't rush right in. She was very careful to prepare for this important discussion. She wasn't manipulative, but she was wise. She knew that "the way to a man's heart is through his stomach" so she prepared an elegant dinner. She didn't merely "spring" the request on him. She had a plan.

She didn't just prepare dinner, but she prepared herself spiritually. She fasted, and she asked others to fast with her. She focused on God for her help. We should seek God's face and prepare ourselves before we counsel with our husband, especially on serious matters.

If there is a matter of correction that we need to discuss, we should be careful to be kind—to say something complimentary before we give the word of correction. Consider how *you* would feel under similar circumstances. "Let your communication be seasoned with salt." And remember the proverb that says, "A word fitly spoken is like apples of gold in pictures of silver" (Prov. 25:11).

Larry Christenson points out that, "The spiritual health and the direction of the family is fully as dependent on the insight and concern of the wife, as upon the authority and protection of the husband."[2]

One's *attitude of the heart* should be a sincere desire to function successfully in this role of helper. A helper must know the philosophies, goals, and desires of the one in charge. She should be in basic agreement with these overarching goals. If she isn't she is headed for a lot of trouble. That issue should be evaluated and settled *before* marriage. It is very unfortunate when these basic issues are clouded over with the blinders of romance. They will rise to haunt you after the honeymoon is over.

Of course, there's plenty of room for differences of opinion underneath these overarching goals and philosophies. In the right attitude and timing a wife may express her differences of opinion and make appropriate appeal. Love may demand that we confront our mate on some issues. If a wise woman remains silent when she believes her husband's decisions are unwise, she may carry a deep and sullen rebellion inside which will harm their relationship and ultimately come out and have to be dealt with.[3]

An intelligent, sensitive, creative wife is a tremendous asset to her husband. But there comes a time when a decision must be made. A wife must then yield to her husband's decision. If she thinks that decision is definitely wrong, she then must make her final appeal to heaven's court—to her God in prayer. If it's a matter that disagrees with God's clear commandments, then she must obey God instead of her husband and trust God with the consequences. "We ought to obey God rather than men" (Acts 5:29). But if it's a matter of taste or judgment in matters that are not of a moral nature, she should sublimate her desires and be supportive of her husband's wishes with God's help.

Of course, a godly husband has the responsibility to pray about these matters and also be sensitive. But we are mainly discussing a wife's responsibilities and the secret to *her* authority. If we are obedient, God will honor and bless our efforts. He may be testing us to see if we just want *our* way or *His* way.

Praying For Those In Authority

I exhort therefore, that, first of all, supplications, prayers, intercessions, and giving of thanks, be made for all men; for kings, and for all that are in authority; that we may lead a quiet and peaceable life in all godliness and honesty. For this is good and acceptable in the sight of God our Saviour (1 Tim. 2:1-3).

It's hard enough to be under the authority of another. Sometimes it becomes almost unbearable if those in authority are unjust, unreasonable, and unloving. I submit to you that prayer is one of the best ways to bring about needed changes. You may not think that this is a concrete enough solution, but it is a method of which God highly approves. Let me illustrate by sharing some ways you can pray for your husband. You can adapt these to others in authority over you.

1. *Spiritually*.

If your husband isn't saved, of course you should pray for his salvation—not so life will be easier for you, but because you desire his spiritual welfare.

If he *is* saved, you should still pray for his spiritual growth. Pray that he will be a man of wisdom, humility, prayer, and compassion. Pray that he will be a Spirit-filled man of God, laying down his rights and learning to take up his cross daily and follow Jesus. If he has a place of leadership in the church, pray for him to be faithful in that position.

2. *Physically.*

Pray that he will exercise discipline in the care of his body—in the things he eats and his exercise. You know his particular weaknesses. Pray for (don't nag) God-given strength in these areas. You can "put feet to your prayers" by fixing nutritious meals and providing an example in the care of your own body.

3. *Mentally.*

Pray that he will be mentally alert and knowledgeable in the areas relevant to his life. Pray about the books and magazines he reads, the TV programs he watches, so that his mind will remain pure.

4. *Emotionally.*

Pray for emotional strength to withstand the pressures that come to him from his job, from his peers, family, and financial conditions.

Pray for emotional compassion—that he will be sensitive to the needs of those he works with, those he lives with, and with those with whom he comes in contact.

5. *Family Life.*

Pray that he will take the spiritual leadership of your

home; that he will take a vital part in teaching the children about the things of God. Pray that he will be an example and a witness to his family. Pray that he will give proper time to his family and that he will teach the right values and priorities by word and example.

6. *Relationships on the job.*

If he is the boss, pray for his ability to administrate, to be fair and sensitive to the needs of his employees. If he is an employee, pray for his diligence, loyalty, and example. If he has a secretary, pray for her and his relationship to her.

7. *Social Relationships.*

Pray for his example and testimony in day-to-day relationships—on the golf course, the tennis court, at the bowling alley, etc. Pray that he will be gracious and courteous, exhibiting an attitude of gentleness like his Savior. One of my favorite Scriptures says, "His gentleness hath made me great" (Ps. 18:35b).

If we *only* pray and are not obeying God's commandments to *us*, then God will not pay attention to our prayers. But if we are obedient and add to this our earnest prayers, God will be faithful and hear and answer our prayers. Many times these answers do not come immediately so we should be persistent in our praying.

God—the Only Perfect Authority

God has ordained authority in our lives. "Let every soul be subject unto the higher powers. For there is no power but of God: the powers that be are ordained of God" (Rom. 13:1). But no human authority is perfect. At some time we will be disappointed by our mother or

father, our husband, some government official, or perhaps even our pastor.

We should be able to expect a higher standard of those
who lead us. The king portrayed in Psalm 45:4 is pictured in this fashion, "And in thy majesty ride prosper-
ously because of *truth* and *meekness* and *righteousness*."
Isaiah 52:11 says, "Be ye clean that bear the vessels of
the Lord." A stricter accountability will be held for those
who are teachers. "Let not many of you become teachers, my brethren, knowing that as such we shall incur a
stricter judgment" (James 3:1, NASB).

Even King David, known as "a man after God's own
heart," slipped into serious sin. He let his wife and family
down. He let his nation down. Most of all he let his God
down, but David repented and God forgave him and
continued to use him, although not without consequences.

Nevertheless, we should be prepared not to be devas-
tated if our leaders make some mistakes. We are to keep
"Looking unto Jesus the author and finisher of our faith
. . . For consider Him . . ." (Heb. 12:2-3). Only God is
perfect, and we cannot expect others to "play God" in
our lives. Many times we expect too much and then feel
let down when those we love and look up to let us down.

Who You Are

You are the One
   in Whom
I find no fault;
All my expectations
   are fulfilled
      in You.

You always keep
　　Your word;
You understand my
　　every need.
You desire to spend
　　Your time
　　　with me;
You remember
　　the words,
　　　the dreams
　　　　we share.

Your gentleness and
　　kindness soothe
　　　my troubled
　　　　brow.
You long to share
　　with me
Your life and
　　love.

You want *me* to
　　understand
　　　Your ways;
You are my beloved
　　and
　　　I am Yours.

I thank You that all I ever dreamed of
in a lover and a leader are perfected in You.
You are my All in All.

　　　　　　　　　　　　—JR

Part III
Women in Ministry

"By Love Serve One Another."

A highly volatile question these days is: *Has God called women into the ministry?* I believe with all my heart that Jesus has called women to minister. Don't misunderstand—I didn't say to be ministers in the commonly accepted sense of the word, that is to be pastors or overseers of the church. But *yes indeed* to minister, to serve our Lord.

I was saved when I was nine years old and even as a teenager I had a deep sense of calling to give my whole life in service to Jesus Christ. I was particularly drawn toward the area of Christian education. I was encouraged by my pastor and his wife, by my Sunday School teacher and Church Training leaders in this desire to serve my Lord. I was a winner in my church and association in the Sword Drill and Better Speakers Tournament.

Several years ago I had a wonderful experience of service. My son David was serving overseas with the missions organization Operation Mobilization. He was in the program division as part of the crew of one of their gospel ships called the *Doulos*. *Doulos* is a Greek word meaning *servant*.

On January the first, Adrian and I met David in West Germany where the ship was then docked. We stayed for several days as guests on the ship and were able to observe the crew firsthand. We were deeply moved with the servant spirit of those on this ship.

Over three hundred young people and adults from forty countries were serving on this ship—giving one, two, and some many more years of their lives. They were living frugally, yes sacrificially, to *serve* their Lord in other lands, sharing the good news of Jesus Christ.

Not only did they share their faith, but they cooked; they cleaned; they painted; they repaired, as well as sang and prayed. When they docked they went into the prisons, the old folks' homes, door to door, businessmen's luncheons, women's Bible studies, into the churches and wherever they could help to distribute Christian literature and to share their faith.

Doulos—"Servant!"

In those days I was deeply challenged once again to minister—to be a *servant* of my Lord and Savior, Jesus Christ.

The Persons Jesus Called into His Ministry

Jesus called *everyone* who loves Him to minister—men and women, young and old, rich and poor alike! But here I want to emphasize that Jesus indeed called women to minister *to* and *for* Him.

New Testament Examples of
Women Who Ministered

1. Jesus chose to come into this world through the portals of a *woman's* womb, the womb of the virgin Mary. We see her *ministering* to Jesus from the day she gave birth in the stable in Bethlehem to the day she stood at the foot of His Cross in Jerusalem, and even beyond.

2. Most of the disciples fled—the Bible says in Matthew 27:55 that "many *women* were there, which followed Jesus from Galilee, *ministering* unto Him."

3. Several *women* were first at the empty tomb, and to whom the angel said, "Go quickly and tell His disciples that He is risen from the dead." Yes, *women* were the very first to tell the "good news."

4. There were *women* who obeyed Jesus and were waiting with the disciples in the upper room for the "promise of the Father."

5. It was a hated Samaritan *woman* to whom Jesus spoke at the well and offered to give her a drink of living water—and that at a time when men didn't speak to women in public, especially to women of her race and reputation.

And it was this *woman* who hurriedly left her waterpot and ran back into the city and said to the men, "Come see a man, who told me everything I ever did: is not this the Christ?"

6. It was a woman—*Lydia,* a seller of purple, who opened her home and said to the apostle Paul in Acts 16:15, "If ye have judged me to be faithful to the Lord, come into my house and abide there."

7. It was a *woman*—Priscilla, who helped her husband instruct Apollos, an eloquent man and mighty in the Scriptures (Acts 18:26).

8. And it was a *woman*—Phoebe, about whom Paul said in Romans 16:1, "I commend unto you Phoebe our sister, which is at Cenchrea."

Other Women in History and Today

Lottie Moon—was the first fully appointed woman missionary of the Foreign Mission Board of the Southern Baptist Convention in 1873. Her example stimulated the development of women's missionary societies. Miss Moon proposed an offering at Christmastime in order to send new women missionaries to relieve her in China, where she had worked without furlough, often alone, for eleven years. Thus the Lottie Moon Christmas offering was named in her honor.[1]

Annie Armstrong—was the founder and the first corresponding secretary of the Woman's Missionary Union of the Southern Baptist Convention in 1888. She is described as a "sharp, forceful, tall, attractive, second generation women's leader, for six years the foremost female advocate for home missions."[2] Her genius was bringing forces together, an ability she recognized as God-given.[3]

However, she "understood Paul's biblical writings in the most literal sense." She refused to speak to mixed groups of men and women.[4]

Betty Stam—along with her husband John, was a missionary to China, sent out by the China Inland Mission, she in 1931 and he in 1932. Married a year later, they labored courageously and were martyred by the Chinese Communists in 1943, displaying an unshakable trust in God.

Thirty hours after their death their precious three-month-old Helen Priscilla Stam was discovered in a deserted house by a traveling Christian, Evangelist Lo. "He found her lying on the bed, just as her mother's hands and heart had planned. Safe in her sleeping bag with its zipper fastened, little Helen was warm and snug, and seemingly none the worse for her long fast. Inside the sleeping bag she had tucked away a clean nightdress and some diapers, all she had been able to bring with her, and among them she had pinned two five-dollar bills.[5]

Betty Stam's parents wrote, "God could no less surely have saved the lives of her precious parents had that been in His divine plan for them."

Bertha Smith—at this writing is ninety-nine years old. "Miss Bertha," as she is lovingly called by all, was appointed by the Foreign Mission Board of the Southern Baptist Convention in 1917. She served in China from 1919 until Communism forced her to leave in 1948. She was there during the great Shantung revival. In 1948 she was transferred to Taiwan as the first missionary of the SBC Foreign Mission Board on that island.

Since her retirement "Miss Bertha" has traveled and spoken extensively throughout our land and has had a profound influence on the lives of multitudes, including my husband and myself.

Corrie Ten Boom—This remarkable woman, who died in the United States at age 90, served time in a German concentration camp during World War II for the "crime" of hiding persecuted Jews, but was sustained by her great faith.

Self-styled "tramp for the Lord," she tirelessly traveled all over the globe for thirty years sharing the reality of Jesus Christ. Her dynamic story was told in her book *The Hiding Place* and portrayed on film under the same title. She won the hearts of the American Christians through sharing her testimony in Billy Graham Crusades.

Mary Slessor—sailed for Nigeria in 1876 and worked there until her death. She fought against witchcraft, drunkenness, twin-killing, and other cruel customs. She believed in "the daily mixing with the people" to break down suspicion and fear. She was extremely fluent in the languages and had an almost uncanny insight into the African mind.

She had an unusual combination of qualities—humor and seriousness, roughness and tenderness, vision and practicality. These, with a cool nerve and disregard for personal health and comfort, helped to make her a powerful influence for Christianity. As a result of her work under God the Ibo people became more Christian than tribes in other parts of Nigeria.

Henrietta Mears—was the inspiration and genius of the great Sunday School of the First Presbyterian Church of Hollywood, California, with its some 6,000 members.

In that Sunday School she herself for many years taught its now famous college class—and administration and teaching gifts do not very often go together.

She was the founder of Gospel Light Publications, which has majored on conservative literature and books. She also saw come into reality her vision of a Bible conference center at Forest Home, where many outstanding Christian leaders were influenced for Christ, including Bill and Vonette Bright, founder and wife of Campus Crusade for Christ.

Her book, *What the Bible Is All About,* has over 1,250,000 in print and has made the Bible come alive and pointed multitudes to see Jesus in every book of the Bible. This book and the story of Miss Mears's life has had a profound impact on my own life.

And there are multitudes of godly women whose names are known to God alone who are *servants* of their Lord. In fact, all of you ladies who know and love Jesus Christ are called . . . called to be *servants,* to minister for your Lord!

The Prerequisites for a Woman's Ministry

Under Authority

There's a big movement on today to show that women are just as intelligent and gifted as men and that a woman can do any job a man can do. My husband says that *everybody* knows that a woman is far superior to a man—at being a woman! And that a man is far superior to a woman—at being a man! But the issue isn't inferior-

ity or superiority. Jesus set straight once for all the mis-
conception caused by sin that women were inferior.

Yes, down through history women *have* been abused,
and even enslaved and treated like property. And *sin* is
the cause! *Sin* causes the man to physically and mentally
abuse the woman, and *sin* also causes the woman to ma-
nipulate and misuse the man. Jesus came to deliver both
the man and the woman who are of equal worth. The
Apostle Paul declares it in Galatians 3:28, ". . . there is
neither male nor female; for ye are all one in Christ
Jesus."

But nowhere did God declare a *sameness of roles!* Oh,
there are individual *tasks* that can be done by either a
man *or* a woman according to who is better gifted to do
that task. For instance, a man or a woman can mow the
yard, cut hair, take out the garbage, keep the checkbook, etc. Many of these tasks have been assigned by
custom, not by Scripture. And frankly, I'm going to stick
with the custom of the man mowing the lawn, although I
know some women who actually enjoy mowing the
grass. If they want to do it that's fine with me. However,
we must learn to divide between custom and the principles of God's Word.

I recently read the story of a Christian woman's strug-
gle with the feeling that her work wasn't considered as
important as the work of a man. She had the feeling that
women, even in the Christian world, were given
"second-class" status. From this feeling she presents the
premise that the curse of the fall has been lifted and that
women have been restored to co-dominion in God's or-

der. She believes, however, that in the home the woman is still to be in submission to her husband, but in "God's kingdom" they are to have "balanced authority." She is a co-pastor with her husband.

I suggest that this lovely lady, sincere as she is, has reached a wrong conclusion through faulty reasoning. First of all, it was Satan who suggested to her that her work wasn't as important as the work of a man. A woman's work certainly *is* as important as a man's work. It is just different. Besides, if she assumes that the work traditionally called women's work is not as important as the man's, then she is suggesting that whoever does that work has a less important job, for someone will have to do those jobs—either a man or a woman.

I have had help from time to time to make my workload easier. But I don't believe the household servant I have employed to help me is inferior. I do not want to give her jobs that are demeaning to her. Cleaning toilets and ironing the clothes may not be my *favorite* thing to do, but I never feel inferior when I do these things. The Bible says, "And whatsoever ye do, do *all* to the glory of God." I've had a special bond of love with those who have helped me through the years. They are special "gifts of God" to me. They are not doing inferior tasks, but helping me with the myriad of mundane tasks that I might be a more relaxed wife and mother.

Secondly, if indeed God had "lifted the curse" and granted co-dominion or equal leadership, I believe it would have applied to the home as well. But I believe that the curse of the fall *has* been lifted, but that the curse was spiritual death. Praise God, through Jesus' death on the Cross I have been set free from the curse of sin and death.

I believe that there were some *consequences* to Adam and Eve's sin that still remain. It is obvious that there are still weeds and thorns in the ground and pain in childbirth. We may not understand or agree, but God allowed these consequences "for thy sake"—for our good. From other Scriptures in the New Testament we have already studied we find that God still has placed the woman *under* man's headship. It is for her protection—for her good.

My husband has an associate pastor whose name is Bob Sorrell. Bob is *under* the authority of my husband. But Bob is God's gift to my husband—to come alongside him, to help, to advise, to gently remind, to help evaluate and organize the many facets of our church. Because Bob is not the pastor of our church doesn't make his function any less important. In fact, our church is so large that my husband could not pastor the church without Bob's valuable help.

Bob knows my husband's heart. He is loyal, diligent, and trustworthy. He has much influence on my husband and thus on the ministry of our church. My husband has delegated to Bob vast areas of responsibilities. But Bob keeps in touch with my husband to make sure that his actions are in keeping with my husband's desires.

How I praise God for this helper, who is also a prized leader. Since he is *under* authority, he has been delegated authority in large areas of our church administration.

Everywhere we go SOMEONE IS IN CHARGE! My husband has said that "anything with two heads is a freak and anything with no head is dead." The buck has to stop somewhere. The Bible isn't a detailed textbook on management, how to be in charge. God allows us to use our creativity and to develop the details in all areas of our lives. But there *are* foundational lines of authority in the Bible for the *ministry of women*. The woman is encouraged—yes, commanded to minister—to *serve*. But she is *not* to take authority over the man. She is to minister *under authority!*

Where does it say that? In God's Word. Let's examine two major passages on this subject.

1 Timothy 2:11,12

> Let the woman quietly receive instruction with entire submissiveness. But I do not allow a woman to teach or exercise authority over a man, but to remain quiet (NASB).

In the sphere of doctrinal disputes or questions of interpretation, where authoritative pronouncements are to be made, the woman is to keep silence. Also in a position of ruling or authority over men, the woman is to remain quiet. If she has questions, the Bible says that she is to ask her husband at home. She is not to be *the* official teacher or doctrine setter of the church.

Some say that this was just the custom of the day.

Granted, some issues *may* relate to custom, but Paul does not appeal to custom, but goes as far back as the Garden of Eden for his explanation. Others say that Paul was prejudiced against women because of his rabbinical training. This view about Paul implies, however, that some parts of the Bible are the word of *man*—not the Word of *God*. And, ladies, the Bible is the Word of *God!*

Some quote male chauvinistic statements made by some ancient rabbis. And I've read some of them—and they *are* atrocious! And even some of the early church fathers were very prejudiced against women.

Oddly enough, those espousing this view will quote the apostle Paul whenever they choose. But you can't have your cake and eat it too, so to speak. You cannot disregard Paul's statements simply because you do not like them. I heard of a young female seminary student who said, "I don't give a _____ what Paul said." Well, ladies I *do* care. I care a whole lot what the apostle Paul says, because I believe that God breathed through him His very Word.

Well, what *did* Paul say? Two simple statements from 1 Timothy 2.

1. Verse 13—"For Adam was first formed, then Eve."

Adam was put in charge by virtue of the *order of creation*.

Is there a commentary we can read on this? Indeed there is! The best commentary I know anything about is the Bible itself. We read in 1 Corinthians 11:8-9, "For the man is not of the woman; but the woman of the man. Neither was the man created for the woman; but the woman for the man." And some male chauvinist didn't think that up. That was *God's original idea*. Paul goes on to say in verses 11 and 12, "Nevertheless neither is the man without the woman, neither the woman without the man, in the Lord. For as the woman is *of* the man, even so is the man also *by* the woman: but all things are of God."

Yes, the man is in charge, not because he is more important or more intelligent, but because that's God's plan for him. Thus he is better suited for this role. But he is not to minister or carry on without the woman's help. She was made to be a suitable helper. He needs her advice and insights. Yes, *some* men say by their actions, "I'll do it all by myself." But God says, "Wait. Don't forget to listen to the helper I gave you." I believe that the classic example of a man who should have listened to the advice of his helper was Pontius Pilate.

2. Verse 14—"And Adam was not deceived, but the woman being deceived was in the transgression."

It clearly states, "The *woman* was deceived." It may have been all the woman's fault, or perhaps Adam failed in *his* responsibility. It just doesn't say! But what it *does* say is that *the woman was deceived*. Some have said that women are being blamed for all the sin in the world. No one is saying this. Yes, the woman *was* the first to sin. But the *Bible* says, "By one *man* sin came into the world" (Rom. 5:12). 1 Corinthians 15:22 says, "As in *Adam* [not Eve] all die . . . ."

Adam was Eve's supervisor. She was deceived, but *he* was *over* her, and he had to take full responsibility for her actions. Now, if Adam wasn't deceived, then *he* sinned with his eyes wide open. There has been a lot of speculation about this. Some say that Adam loved Eve so much that he couldn't bear to be without her, so he willingly sinned. Others have said that Adam is a type of Christ and that he took her sins that she might be redeemed. *It doesn't clearly say!*

God has given her the man for a covering—a protection! Is she more emotional in her nature, and thus more susceptible to false doctrine? *It doesn't clearly say this either,* so we can only speculate. But 2 Timothy 3:5-7 *does* state,

> In the last days perilous times shall come . . . . Having a form of godliness, but denying the power thereof: from such turn away. For of this sort are they which creep into houses, and lead captive silly women laden with sins, led away with divers lusts, ever learning, and never able to come to the knowledge of the truth.

This passage *does* say that in the last days there shall be:

> Gullible women: "they lead captive silly women"
> Guilty women: "laden with sins"
> Greedy women: "led away with divers lusts"
> Grasping women: "ever learning, and never able to come to the knowledge of the truth"

1 Corinthians 14:34-35

> Let your women keep silence in the churches for it is not permitted unto them to speak, but they are commanded to be under obedience [under authority] as

also saith the law. And if they will learn anything, let them ask their husbands at home; for it is a shame for women to speak in the church.

The word silence can be translated "quietness." In other words this doesn't necessarily mean that a woman cannot say a word, but that she shouldn't be bossy, wanting to take control—but should have a "meek and quiet spirit."

Paul says in 1 Corinthians 11:5 and verses 13-15 that a woman may pray or prophesy *if* she has her head covered. What the literal head covering was has been debated by godly people down through the ages. Some say it was a veil or hat. Others say it is long hair. Still others say that it is hair *long enough* and in an appropriate style to show the difference between the man and the woman. It *may* have been a custom, and customs may change. But regardless of *how* you interpret it, the meaning does not change. I believe that the meaning behind the symbol is clear. It shows a woman's willingness to be *under authority*.

Men in the Church

Let me now make a few statements about the examples and statements in God's Word which show that *men* should be in charge in the area of the ministry.

- All of the writers of the Bible were men.
- All of the apostles were men.
- The pastors of the New Testament churches were men.

- When the qualifications for pastors and deacons were given they were given for men.

Some guidelines for a pastor are found in 1 Timothy 3.

- He is to be the *husband* of one wife.
- He is to be "one who rules well *his* own house, having *his* children in subjection. For if a *man* know not how to rule *his* own house, how shall *he* take care of the church of God?"
- He should be in charge at church as well as at home. *If he* doesn't rule well at home, then he shouldn't be in charge at church.

There are some who move heaven and earth trying to show that women should have *equal* leadership roles. This is called an egalitarian philosophy. For instance, they say that Phoebe was a deaconess. Well, she was, in the sense that she was a *servant* of the church. Deacon (or deaconess) means *servant*. In that sense *I* am a deaconess—a *servant* of Bellevue Baptist Church. But nowhere does it say she was part of an official body of deacons who were appointed and assigned to specific duties in the church. This body is made up of men.

One verse used by both sides to prove their point is Galatians 3:28: "There is neither Jew nor Greek, there is neither bond nor free, there is neither male nor female: for ye are all one in Christ Jesus."

Yes, I believe this verse with all my heart. I believe it proves once and for all that women *aren't* inferior. Certainly the apostle Paul didn't teach the inferiority of the woman, but some have *falsely* interpreted his teachings to mean this. We have already seen that submission does *not* mean inferiority.

But even some of the early church fathers wrongly interpreted Paul's teaching and taught that the woman was inferior. But just because these men misinterpreted God's Word on this issue does not validate another wrong teaching.

Galatians 3:28 shows that women are of equal *worth* in God's sight to men. I don't have to stand in line behind any man to share my requests with my Heavenly Father. But nowhere does this verse guarantee *sameness* of function and equality of roles.

Some say that men being in charge was simply the custom of *that* day. But Jesus wasn't afraid to break customs if they went against God's Word.

- He healed on the sabbath—and was accused of being a sabbath-breaker.
- He spoke to the woman at the well—when the custom of that day said not to.

No, it went *beyond* custom to a great underlying principle of who *God* put in charge. You may think that it is demeaning, like being assigned to be a second-rate citizen, so to speak. Certainly not!

God made you with a different purpose, a different role. You were not made to be a king but to live like a *queen!* And in that place of submission, your ministry can be far-reaching. It is a place of counsel, a place of help. The one in charge needs a trusted, prized person to be his helper. Yours is a place of delegated authority.

You Are Indeed a Queen!

A queen rules also—she just rules *under authority*. And when the "king" delegates his authority to you in some area, you can carry on backed by *his* authority.

You mothers, you are queens in your homes. Jack Hyles said that you may have a

> Needle—for a scepter
> Righteousness—for your robe
> The Needy—for your subjects
> Meekness—for a crown.

What is that in *your* hand? What is *your* scepter?

> Is it a ROLLING PIN or A WOODEN SPOON?
> Then *pick it up and rule* from the kitchen!
> Is it a THERMOMETER?
> Then *pick it up and rule* from the bedside!
> Is it a BALLPOINT PEN?
> Then *pick it up and rule* from your desk!

In the home, a woman rules those who are to rule the world. She can be the queen of kings. With her willingness to serve with a meek and quiet spirit, she rules the hearts of men. What is in your hand? Well, *pick it up and rule!*

Yes, many women are excellent speakers, good at administration, and highly gifted. God wants those women to speak, to use their gift of organization, to use their creativity. But He wants them to do it *under authority* and in accordance with His guidelines.

Some are claiming that God calls women to be pastors, and *if* He does that *we* should allow them to do it—

that they have the ability and availability. But the issue is not ability or availability, but *authority*. What does God's Word say? It's not what *we* think or what *we* feel, but what God's Word says.

- Sarah was the mother of the Jewish nation. She did it by being UNDER AUTHORITY.
- Queen Esther saved an entire nation, but she did it by being UNDER AUTHORITY.
- Ruth, a Gentile bride, was placed in the genealogy of Jesus Christ. She did it by being UNDER AUTHORITY.
- Huldah was a prophetess, but she did it UNDER AUTHORITY.

Proper Priority

First of all, let me make it clear that we minister in *every* sphere of our lives: in our homes and communities, in our neighborhoods and our churches, *wherever* we go!

Ministry is not limited to activities in and through the church, so none of us is ever exempt from ministry. But the sphere and the extent of your ministry depends upon the proper priority in your individual life.

God's Word makes it very plain in 1 Corinthians 7:34 that the single woman and the married woman have a different set of priorities. The woman who is called by God to a life of singleness can have a unique relationship to her Lord. The central focus of her life can be to please her Lord (1 Cor. 7:32). There will be more time to be alone with God, more time for sharing with others about

Jesus and ministering to those who are suffering. But everyone is not called to this kind of life. Paul says that "every man hath his proper gift of God." Obviously, the single life, even of service, is not meant for everyone, or there would not be a human race. God has called some very special people to be single for the kingdom of God (Matt. 19:12).

Some married women today are trying their best to do away with their God-assigned priorities. They want so-called equality not only with men but also with their single sisters. They want to enjoy the benefits of marriage and family without the priorities attached. They want to relieve the mother of the priority of childcare. Some have encouraged abortion (they call it "freedom of choice") not only for the unwed mother, but also for the married woman who doesn't want children to interfere with her career.

What are some factors in determining the *sphere* and *extent* of a *married* woman's ministry? Are you fulfilling GOD'S CHIEF ASSIGNMENT as stated in Titus 2:5 to be "keepers at home"? Let me give you a little quiz to see if you are.

- What are the desires of your husband; the number and ages of your children?
- Do you keep your home clean and attractive?
- Do you provide nutritious meals in a relaxed atmosphere?
- Do you keep your family attractively and neatly clothed?

- Do you take time to be a thrifty shopper?
- Do you keep yourself rested so you can have a meek and quiet spirit?
- Are you hospitable to your family and friends, reaching out to those in physical and spiritual need?
- Do you take time to train your children, to fellowship with them, to encourage them and be involved in their activities?
- Do you make time to keep yourself attractive and interesting—being an encourager and a lover to your husband?
- Do you strive to *excel* instead of just getting by at being a wife, mother, and homemaker?

This is your chief assignment from God. When you have fulfilled this assignment you may then extend the sphere of your ministry in consultation with your husband and communion with your God.

I know some of you are single parents and out of great necessity must leave your children to provide the necessities of life. My hat is off to you, and my blessings are upon you! If you must work, there are multitudes of opportunities for you to minister day by day where you work or play.

The Practice of a Woman's Ministry

I want to give six examples of New Testament women for you to follow as you seek to minister for the Lord under authority.

1. Work at Being Winsome with the Woman at the Well

> The woman then left her waterpot, and went her way into the city, and saith to the men, Come, see a man, which told me all things that ever I did: is not this the Christ? (John 4:28-29).

This woman was someone who simply went back to those she knew and told what she had seen and heard. We must note, however, that she had experienced a change in her life and that her experience with the Lord had power to draw people to Christ. Notice that it didn't say she told the women but that she told the men about Jesus. She obviously would not have been received by the women. But she went where and to whom she could with her life-changing message—"Come see a man . . . is not this the Christ?"

Someone is waiting to hear what God has done for you. Go first to those who know you best, to your family, your friends, to the people with whom you work. Go first even to those with whom you've sinned. Some will see and respond to the changed life they witness firsthand. If they will not receive the message of life, then tell it to whomever will listen. Tell about Christ to your beautician, to your dentist, to the service station attendant, to the bag boy at the grocery store. Tell it on your job, in the classroom, at the PTA meeting. Win some with the woman at the well. I remember a little chorus we sang at my church when I was just a little girl. It was entitled, "Win Them One by One."

If to Christ our only King
We desire some soul to bring
Just one way may this be done
We must win them one by one.

If you bring the one next to you
And I bring the one next to me
In all kinds of weather
We'll all work together
And see what can be done.

If you bring the one next to you
And I bring the one next to me
In no time at all
We'll win them all
So win them, win them
One by one.

2. Learn a Lesson from Lydia

And on the sabbath we went out of the city by a river side, where prayer was wont to be made; and we sat down, and spake unto the women which resorted thither. And a certain woman named Lydia, a seller of purple, of the city of Thyatira, which worshiped God, heard us whose heart the Lord opened, that she attended unto the things which were spoken of Paul. And when she was baptized, and her household, she besought us, saying, If ye have judged me to be faithful to the Lord, come into my house, and abide there. And she constrained us (Acts 16:13-15).

Lydia used her home to serve her Lord. She invited Paul to stay at her house and shared her provisions with him. What a blessing comes to those who will open their hearts and homes to God's servants. There is no better way to influence your children for godliness than to have in your home men and women who are Spirit-filled servants of God.

Besides offering hospitality to God's servants there are a variety of ways to open your home as a witness for Christ. Start right in your neighborhood. Invite your neighbors to supper or for a time of fellowship or Bible study.

A good way to reach out to the ladies in your neighborhood is to have a neighborhood evangelistic tea. Have delicious refreshments and beautiful flowers and invite your neighbors over for a time of fellowship. You can invite a friend to share her testimony of what Christ means in her life. There are various ways of sharing Christ so as not to be offensive.

Or perhaps you might want to start with a time of fellowship and open the door to go back later. Another possibility is to have a Backyard Bible Club for the children in your neighborhood. Be sure always to be up front with what you are doing.

3. Discern what Dorcas Did

Now there was at Joppa a certain disciple named Tabitha, which by interpretation is called Dorcas: this woman was full of good works and almsdeeds which she did . . . Then Peter arose and went with them. When he was come, they brought him into the upper chamber: and all the widows stood by him weeping, and shewing the coats and garments which Dorcas made, while she was with them (Acts 9:26,29).

Dorcas was an able seamstress who used her creativity to minister to others. In Bellevue Baptist Church there is a sewing group which meets every week and gives of its time to sew stuffed animals for the children who are in the pediatrics wing of Baptist Hospital here in Memphis. Then they sew little carriers made in the shapes of valentines for those babies who go home on Valentine's Day.

With these gifts made by loving hands also is given a New Testament and a little book. These are meant to be a witness for our Lord. Very few people visit the sewing room, but God meets with them on Tuesdays. He knows, and He blesses these "cups of cold water" given in His name.

Perhaps you say, "I can't sew." Well, can you bake bread? Then take a freshly baked loaf to that neighbor and tell her about Jesus, the Bread of Life! Do you have a "green thumb" and can you grow beautiful flowers? Take a bouquet to a sick friend and share with her about Jesus, the Rose of Sharon.

Can you cross-stitch or paint? I remember some years ago when my daughter Janice was pregnant with her first child and was very sick a good deal of the time. She took up cross-stitching to ease the "misery." The husband of a good friend died, and Janice had the idea of cross-stitching the Bible verse, "Weeping may endure for a night, but joy cometh in the morning" (Ps. 30:5b). She said, "Mother, if you will pay for the frame, I will do the stitching." I said, "It's a deal." Mary Hunter was so blessed and touched by this gift from her young friend that it developed a closeness that still continues through the years. Can you write a poem or sing a song? Use that talent to minister to someone who is lonely or sad.

4. *Pursue Priscilla's Plan*

And he began to speak boldly in the synagogue: whom when Aquila and Priscilla had heard, they took him unto them, and expounded unto him the way of God more perfectly (Acts 18:26).

Priscilla was a real helper to her husband. She joined in with Aquila to help Apollos better understand God's ways. Many times as I've been along when my husband visited the hospital or a home, God has given me just the right word of encouragement or comfort. On occasion when we've been standing around a bedside at a crisis hour, Adrian has asked me to sing a song, and God has richly anointed me on these occasions to communicate a message from Him in the simplest of ways. A favorite of his that he will frequently ask me to sing is a simple Scripture song:

> They that trust in the Lord
> shall be as Mount Zion
>   Which cannot be removed
> but abideth forever.
>
>   As the mountains are round
> about Jerusalem
>   So the Lord is round about
> His people,
>   So the Lord is round about

His people
From henceforth forever.
(Psalm 125:1-2)

If your husband is also a Christian, you can share hospitality together. Open your home to have dinner with another couple or have a small or large group. It just depends on how large your home is and your own desires and style.

One Christmas we were living in a brand-new neighborhood in a new city. No one on our street knew who we were. We decided to have a neighborhood family open house. We sent out invitations and at the bottom wrote these words: "We will share the true meaning of Christmas." At a good point in the evening, we gathered in the living room around the piano and sang Christmas carols. A friend sang a couple of well-loved Christmas songs, and then my husband shared some brief thoughts about what Christmas meant to us. They still didn't know that evening that my husband was a new minister in town, but they found out soon. The Lord used us in that neighborhood to reach out while we lived there.

You can always invite friends to go to church with you. At our church we have several outstanding musical dramas each year, and this provides a wonderful opportunity to open up our hearts and our church to these friends.

Our church provides many opportunities to be personally involved in sharing the gospel in other parts of the United States and overseas, as well as in our own city. I have had the privilege on several occasions to go with my husband and share in this ministry—singing, giving a testimony, praying, and visiting in the homes with national Christians. This has been one of the highlights of my life. In addition, God has implanted in my heart a vision for the world. I feel such a oneness in my heart with these fellow Christians from different parts of the world. I can see their faces now—lovely Christians in Taiwan, Korea, Italy, Israel, West Germany, and other places of the world.

5. *Emulate Eunice's Example*

When I call to remembrance the unfeigned faith that is in thee, which dwelt first in thy grandmother Lois, and thy mother Eunice; and I am persuaded that is in thee also (2 Tim. 1:15).

Eunice influenced young Timothy by her life of genuine faith. Don't let someone else have the joy of leading your children to Christ. How wonderful it has been to teach my children, to sing to them, and to know that partly through my influence they came to know the Lord.

I now have the joy of seeing this faith multiplied in the lives of my children as I see them teaching their children the things of the Lord. How exciting it was when my oldest granddaughter, Renae, was learning the "ABCs Bible Memory Plan." She was learning at age five a verse that started with every letter in the alphabet. And when Angela was four years old, my daughter Janice taught her to answer the phone this way, "'This is the day that the Lord hath made. Let us rejoice and be glad in it.' This is Angela Brock, May I help you please?"

Walking along the beach, I've sung to my grandchildren the same song I sang to my children, "Oh, who can make the seashells? I'm sure I can't, can you? No one can make the seashells. No one but God, 'tis true!"

Then just a few weeks ago I experienced one of the greatest joys of my life. We made a special trip to Florida to witness the baptism of our first grandchild, Renae. What a thrill for "Grammy" to be able to take video pictures as her granddaddy put her under the baptismal waters. I gave her a very special Jerusalem Cross, that I had purchased in the Holy Land, to remember that significant occasion.

Just yesterday I wrote down some Scripture references about singing and praising and sent them to my son, Steve, who is a minister of music in Florida. I just wanted him to share in some of my discoveries that had blessed my life. Some of the training and discipline has stopped since my children are grown, but I will keep on ministering and encouraging as long as I live.

6. *Follow the Faith of Phoebe*

I commend unto you Phoebe our sister, which is a servant of the church which is at Cenchrea: that ye receive her in the Lord, as becometh saints, and that ye assist her in whatsoever business she hath need of you: for she hath been a succourer of many, and of myself also" (Rom. 16:1-2).

Phoebe was a faithful servant of the church. She didn't have to be the pastor to be greatly used of God. I have been a servant of the church for many, many years. We as women can teach women and children in Sunday School, lead youth groups, work with the needy, serve in the Women's Ministry, invite the unsaved to churchwide events, serve on committees, decorate for luncheons or special events, arrange flowers, serve in the nursery, open our homes to entertain special guests of the church, sing in the choir, and a multitude of other things.

Whatever your circumstances, God has called *you* into *His* ministry. He just wants you to minister *under authority* and with the *proper priority*.

Part IV

Women's Role Today

Feminism, I believe, is not synonymous with femininity or being lady-like. Feminism indicates a desire to be equal with men in their role or function, and it involves a resistance against commonly accepted traditional roles.

The secular feminist crusades for *equal rights* because she has not experienced the equality of worth she gains when she is in Christ. Without spiritual perception she is not able to discern between God's established principles, man-made customs, and sin-related abuses, so she cannot arrive at the correct solution to her problems.

With a spirit of love for my sisters in Christ, I want us to deal with the problems of feminism. We will look at the *secular feminists'* position, so a Christian woman can be aware of this philosophy and make sure she is not unknowingly emulating this point of view in lesser ways.

The Christian woman should also be aware that there are those who call themselves *biblical feminists*. They certainly do not fall into the category of the *secular feminists*. However, I would differ with biblical feminists in their outlook on the nature of Holy Scripture and its interpretation.

We must recognize there are varying degrees of this

position, and that everyone claiming to be a biblical feminist may not agree with all of the positions of those on the far left of this approach.

It is obvious, however, when scanning bibliographies on this subject, that the major resource material has come from more radical biblical feminists outside the ranks of conservative evangelicals in general. Most evangelical Christian women, and even many pastors, are not aware of the beliefs of the biblical feminists and where this philosophy could lead.

Legitimate Concerns

I do not deny that there have been and are serious problems related to the treatment of women. Indeed, if there were no legitimate problems, there would be no extreme feminist movement. Down through the ages women have been taken advantage of, sexually abused, and even enslaved because of their lesser physical strength. Sometimes men feel threatened by strong-willed or highly intelligent women.

God originally designed the woman to be a highly esteemed helper or associate. In many cases she has been denied this position, and her duties have been limited to menial tasks only. Often the woman has not been appreciated for her God-given abilities and insights but has been ridiculed for not behaving or thinking like a man. In an attempt to make her over into the male likeness, many men won't necessarily like the end result. She will lose some of her gentleness and sensitivity.

The woman may not realize it, but she may unconsciously be attempting to measure up to the qualities she sees the man admire. Perhaps he would not admit it, but his lack of appreciation for the woman's uniquely God-given qualities may have driven her to emulate the male-appreciated qualities.

There are all degrees of problems related to the treatment of women. Some women have been grievously abused—mentally and/or physically. They have been put down, knocked down, cursed, or neglected. Others have been mildly mistreated or simply ignored. Many women are starved for attention from a man who sits in front of the television or hides behind his newspaper night after night.

Abuses of Women

It's not all the fault of the men, however. *Why* do they put down, knock down, or curse their women? Sometimes could it be partially the fault of wives who do not admire their husbands, who belittle, who are status seekers pushing their husbands to "keep up with the Joneses"? Could it be the fault of women who are manipulative and selfish? I am merely asking.

Indeed many a woman dreads the drudgery of washing, ironing, meal preparation, and the constant care of children with hardly a bathroom break. There is little appreciation for these thankless tasks, and at the end of most days, she is so tired she feels like falling into bed instead of being romantic.

However, the woman is so often caught up in the "myriad of the mundane" that she forgets to admire her man's accomplishments and to soothe his troubled brow. Men *and* women often forget the "dignity of drudgery" and that nothing really worthwhile is gained without hours of routine—whether it's becoming a brain surgeon, a concert pianist, or raising godly children.

The abuses and misuses of men *and* women are related to that little three-letter word *sin*. Right in the middle of that word is the key to our problem—the big I. Selfishness is a sin problem and is at the center of all male-female problems. But clamoring for *equal rights* is not the answer. I feel this only produces masculine-like women. The softness of femininity has been rubbed off.

The only answer to the *sin* problem is Jesus Christ. Only as we lay our selfish rights at His feet are we able to rebuild *right* relationships with the opposite sex.

Pressures

Pressures have arisen from some feminist ranks to eliminate the commonly accepted biblical interpretation of the woman's role in the home and in the church. One example of this is the National Organization for Women. In its official booklet called, *Revolution: Tomorrow Is Now,* the following resolution appears:

"In the light of the enslavement of body and mind which the church historically has imposed on women, we demand that the seminaries:

a. Immediately stop and repudiate their propagation of sexist, male supremist doctrine,

b. Initiate women's study courses which cut through the traditional male, religious mythology to expose church and other social forces denying women their basic human dignity,

c. Actively recruit, employ, and justly promote women theologians and other staff in all departments,

d. Actively recruit, enroll, financially aid, and seek equal placement for women theological students."[1]

Secular feminism does not look to God's Word and His wisdom to deal with the problems related to the treatment of women. It looks to human wisdom and therefore arrives at wrong conclusions.

Assuming to know what equality is, the feminist seeks to attain it by her own ingenuity. Thinking this means she should be able to work at any job a man can, she seeks to free herself of any seeming incumbrances that would prevent her from attaining this goal.

This entails freeing herself from unwanted pregnancies and the daily so-called drudgery of childcare. Thus she may justify abortion. Aiming to succeed in the male-oriented work place she either postpones marriage and childbearing or neglects these God-assigned priorities for a woman's life.

Sometimes those women who have been rejected, neglected, or abused by men turn to lesbian relationships in an attempt to find acceptance and tenderness. But failing to find her guidance from God's Word she distorts God's purpose for her life, misusing even God-intended female friendships.

The *extreme* feminist is also a humanist. Tim LaHaye in his book, *The Battle for the Mind,* says that, "Humanism is a man-centered philosophy that attempts to solve the problems of man and the world independently of God."[2] It is not just being humanitarian or humane. We might say that, "It is the wisdom of man." He continues, "Humanism is not only the world's greatest evil but, until recently, the most deceptive of all religious philosophies."[3]

We read the story of the wise man who built his house on a rock (Matt. 7:24-27). When the winds, rains, and floods came his house stood, for it was built on a sure foundation. On the other hand the foolish man built *his* house on the sand. When the winds, rains, and floods came *his* house fell because it had a *faulty foundation.*

Why does a man build a house? He wants protection from the elements. The rains bring *pressures from above;* the winds bring *pressures from without;* the floods bring *pressures from beneath.*

What does this mean to us? We need protection so we must build on a sure foundation. In today's world there are two major conflicting philosophies upon which we are building our lives—either the solid Rock of God's Word or the shifting sands of humanism.

The humanists have five destructive tenets on which they are building their lives.

1. *Atheism.*

The foundation stone of all humanistic thought is atheism—the belief that there is no God. "As nontheists, we begin with humans, not God, nature not deity. Promises of immortal salvation or fear of eternal damnation are illusory and harmful."[4]

But God's Word declares, "The fool hath said in his heart, there is no God" (Ps. 14:1). But I *know* that my Redeemer lives. He is the Living Word of God. Jesus Christ is Lord and *He is God* (Phil. 2:6,11; John 1:3).

2. *Evolution*.

The teaching that man evolved is the primary foundation on which all secular education rests. Much of this thinking even permeates many "Christian" schools and universities. On June 20, 1987, the Supreme Court struck down a ruling of the Louisiana Supreme Court that required creation-science to be given equal teaching with evolution in the public schools.

God's Word declares, "In the beginning God *created* the heaven and the earth" (Gen. 1:1). Adam didn't evolve. God's Word says that he was created in the image of God (Gen. 1:26).

3. *Amorality*.

Next follows that there are no absolutes when it comes to morality. "Ethics is autonomous and situational, needing no theological or ideological sanction. . . . Reason and intelligence are the most effective instruments that humankind possesses. There is no substitute, neither faith nor passion suffice in itself."[5]

God's Word says that there are absolutes—unchangeable commandments—morality issued from God Himself. The Bible however, is a book of great principles, not minute laws about each and every detail. God indeed allows man to think and search for *daily* guidance.

4. *An Autonomous, Self-Centered Man*.

The next logical conclusion for the humanist is an autonomous, self-centered man, with unlimited goodness and potential if his environment is controlled to let his free spirit develop.

Frances Schaeffer pointed out that "autonomous thinking" historically does not lead to world betterment but to chaos. The humanists emphasize *feeling* rather than responsibility. "If it *feels* good, it must *be* good." Do your own thing. Selfishness pervades this country as never before. The "I want *my* way" individual will seek to get rather than give, lust rather than love, demand rather than contribute. This all leads to hostility and war.

5. *A One-World Government.*

The humanist believes in a one-world government.

> We deplore the division of humankind on nationalistic grounds. We have reached a turning point in human history where the best option is to transcend the limits of national sovereignty and to move toward the building of a world community in which all sectors of the human family can participate."[6]

This may sound good on the surface, but without *God* as the ruler this will produce the epitome of what man can do without God—and it won't be good.

God's Word says that Christ's kingdom will come, when all those who know and love God will follow our King, Jesus. There will be no more war. The swords will be turned into pruning hooks. The lion will lie down with the lamb (Isa. 11:6).

Some secular feminists have as an aim by the year

2000 to believe in human potential, not God. The Bible is viewed as a sexist book; and the biblical roles of male headship and a woman's submission are viewed as oppressive. Their understanding of these concepts is only viewed through their limited experiences of abuses or misuses of these God-given roles. Sin causes a man to be dictatorial, self-serving, and abusive instead of being the loving servant-leader and protector he was intended to be.

To correct this distorted view the mistreated woman should look to the role models God gives. First and foremost God's Son, the Lord Jesus Christ, epitomizes the loving servant-leader-protector. We then must look at those men in whom Jesus Christ is living to see these principles practiced. No one but Jesus is perfect, but we can see His likeness shining through in men attempting to live the Spirit-filled life.

Much of the courtesy and protection that came as a result of male headship is diminished by supposed equal rights, i.e. men holding the door for a woman or giving up his seat in her behalf, common niceties. Some are wanting equality in military combat and on the police force. They want higher paid jobs in addition to equal admiration. They think that this adds up to fulfillment— but they are finding it is not always so.

Many of the goals of the humanists are those of all mankind. *They* want love, peace, self-worth, provision, and protection, but they have denied and scorned the Word of God, Who is *infinite* love and *everlasting* peace, the One who gives self-worth and identity, Who is our Provider and Who is our Refuge and Strength.

Then what *is* the answer to the storms of life, the swirling winds of change, the torrential rains of adversity, and the floodtides of doubt and despair? We as Christians can't deny the discrimination and abuse of the poor, women, children, and minority groups. We can't deny the problems of unwanted pregnancies, drug abuse, perversion, power-hungry men and women, and war. We can't deny that our resources are being wasted and that crime is on the upsurge. We're both afraid to stay at home and afraid to go out of our houses. We can't deny that some in the world live under totalitarian governments that suppress freedom, that dehumanize personality. No, we can't hide our *heads in the sand like an ostrich* and hope that these storms will blow away.

What will we Christians do? What can we offer to the world? We must build our lives and the lives of our families on the *sure foundation of God's Word.* We must tell our neighbors, our friends, the ungodly, yes, the humanists that the answer to the storms of life is the Word of God.

> JESUS—the Living, powerful Word of God!
> THE BIBLE—the written Word of God!

They are inseparable. United in your life they are the solid rock which will cause your house, your life to stand.

Remember that in Matthew 7 there were *two* houses. The winds, the rains, and the floods beat upon both houses. Being a Christian and trusting in *His* Word doesn't make us immune to the storms of life. I've personally been in the floodtides of sorrow. As the rains and winds beat upon my life, when the floods tried to over-whelm me, I held onto the Solid Rock, and my house has withstood the storm.

> On Christ, the Solid Rock I stand
> All other ground is sinking sand;
> All other ground is sinking sand.

Yes, God's Word is the basis for a woman's authority. If she submits her life to this authority, she will have a sure foundation for her life. *God's instructions* are given in His Word. If it were not for God's *written* Word, we would not know what He wants us to be and do.

What kind of book is the Bible? It is a *precious* book! There are many similes given for this most priceless of books.

Your Precious Word

Your Word is like a lamp
It guides me when I
cannot see my way.

Your Word is like a seed
It must be planted in my life
so it can grow.

Your Word is like a sword
It divides between my judgment
and
the wisdom that
comes from You.

Your Word is like a mirror
Showing me what I'm
really like inside.

Your Word is like milk
    Giving me daily sustenance
        that I might live.

Your Word is sweeter than honey
    It's the only remedy when
        my spirit turns sour.

Your Word is more precious than gold
    Its worth does not compare
        to this world's goods.

I do not doubt Your Word
    for it is settled forever
        in heaven (Ps. 119:89).

I love Your Word so I
    think on it all
        through the day (Ps. 119:97).

I prize Your Word for it
    teaches me to love right
        and hate wrong (Ps. 119:128).

I hope in Your Word for
    it is steadfast and
        pure (Ps. 119:140).

I rejoice at Your Word for
    it is a precious
        treasure (Ps. 119:162).

Your commandments are faithful (Ps. 119:86).

Your judgments are right (Ps. 119:75).

Your testimonies are everlasting (Ps. 119:144).

When I am sad it
    brings me comfort.
When I am in danger it
    gives me hope.

When I am sick it
  soothes my brow.
When I am lost it
  brings me home.

I will meditate in Your precepts (Ps. 119:78)

I will love Your law (Ps. 119:97)

I will delight in Your statutes (Ps. 119:16)

I will remember Your judgments (Ps. 119:52)

I will believe Your commandments (Ps. 119:66)

  I will keep Your Word
    for it is my delight.

  I am Your servant
    I will not forget
      Your law.

                              —JR

Costly Trends

In *The Wall Street Journal* Joann S. Lublin wrote that
"gaps are narrowing between the sexes in alcoholism, suicide, crime, and even car crashes. Some are pointing to
added stresses related to female "emancipation." Federal
health officials estimate that one of every three Ameri-
cans with a drinking problem is a woman compared with
only one of six a decade ago.

In the wake of the revolution in sex roles and gains in
female employment, women are increasingly afflicted by
a range of social and physical problems that used to be
largely the domain of men. It is a phenomenon that some
describe—in a much-disputed analysis—as 'the dark side
of female emancipation.'"[7]

Alice Rossi, a University of Massachusetts sociology professor, says that "when you break the homebound nature of women's lives and get them into jobs then you're bound to get an elevation of their drinking, smoking, and accident rates."[8] Many feminists disagree that women's liberation is to blame for their increasing ills. Evaluate some of the statistics for yourself.

Cigarette use. Smoking by males has dropped considerably while female consumption has remained steady. It is now estimated that more teenage girls smoke than boys. It is shocking to realize that lung cancer has overtaken breast cancer in the mid-1980s as the leading killer of females.

Heart Disease. Since 1968 deaths from heart disease have been declining faster for men than women. (Believed to reflect changing patterns of smoking. May also indicate job stress.)

A recent study by the National Heart, Lung, and Blood Institute found that middle-aged mothers dissatisfied with their office and sales positions were twice as likely to develop heart disease as housewives.

Suicide. The gap is narrowing between men and women, although twice as many men as women still take their own lives.

Longevity. An average American woman lives eight years longer than the average man. The gap widened by a year per decade from 1900-1970. In the 1970s women's longevity slowed, and some social scientists think that women's life expectancy will not be increasing.

"Women are starting to behave like men; pretty soon, we ought to see their death rates look like those of men," says Lois Verbrugge, a biostatistics professor at the University of Michigan's School of Public Health.

Crime. Women's involvement in such crimes as embezzlement, fraud, and forgery is rising sharply in the United States. Of these crimes, only one in six was committed by a woman in 1960. By 1977 that rose to one in three. (Today the statistics are close to 2.5.) Rita Simon, a University of Illinois sociology professor, suggests that women with jobs have more opportunity to steal.[9]

You be the judge! Do you think that as women's roles grow more like men's so do their problems? Is the cost worth the so-called equality?

Another cost of equality is the loss of femininity. In a recent article in our local newspaper the headline was "Accent is on Management." This is what followed:

> There's only one way for women to get to the top: forget they are women. At least that's the conclusion of one woman who conducted 300 interviews for her book on working for a female boss.
>
> Trash femininity, stop baking brownies and nix plans for babies. Because the nature of leadership is unchangeable, "women must become clones of men" if they are to make it to the chief executive's suite, said author Dr. Paula Bern.
>
> Women have to emulate the skills many see as masculine—decisiveness, aggressiveness, assertiveness and willingness to take risks," she said.
>
> Although 37 percent of the nation's managers are

women, "at the top echelon, there are zero," said Dr. Bern, author of *How to Work for a Woman Boss, Even if You'd Rather Not.*[10]

The chief problem in discussing biblical feminism, I feel, is an inability to divide correctly between biblical principles, sin-related abuses, and man-made customs. Biblical principles are unchanging. Sin-related abuses are always wrong, and man-made customs may be good, bad, or just outdated.

Biblical Principles

To establish biblical principles one must first determine her view of the nature of Holy Scripture. Norman L. Geisler and William Nix briefly explain the three major views about the place of the Bible in God's revelation:

1. The *Liberal* view is that the Bible contains the Word of God, along with the words and errors of men. This view is based upon a naturalistic premise. It makes human reason and feeling the final judges of revelation, and it does not take seriously what the Bible has to say about itself.

2. The *Neoorthodox* view is that the Bible *becomes* the Word of God in an existential experience, when its message becomes meaningful to the individual. This position is too subjective. It is also based on a naturalistic premise. It furthermore ignores the fact that the Bible is not only a record of personal revelations, but that it is itself a propositional revelation.

3. The *Conservative* view is that the Bible *is* the written Word of God. It holds that Bible to be God's objective

revelation whether or not man has a subjective illumination of it.[11]

Some claim that conservatives believe in Mechanical Dictation—that God dictated the words and that men were just scribes or as some say, "religious robots." This theory is probably a "straw man" since no one of reputation lays claim to this belief.

Others hold the *Dynamic* view, which localizes inspiration in the concepts or ideas, that the writers were free to express God's ideas in their own way. The essential objection to the inspired concept theory is that it is *linguistically impossible*. In order for God to give full expression of His thoughts to man, He had to use man's symbols or language. God gave the idea, yet it was given in *man's words*.[12]

"*The Basic biblical view:* The *Verbal Plenary* view. The third alternative, and the one that is biblical (to me), is that all the words (verbal) which are written are God-breathed (2 Tim. 3:16). God gave full (plenary) expression to His thought in the words of the biblical record. He guided in the very choice of words used within the personality and the cultural complex of the writers so that, in some inscrutable manner, the Bible is the Word of God while being the words of men.

"The end product is as authoritative as if it were mechanically dictated, but as writer-orientated as if it were humanly created. The means is *dynamic,* and the end result is authoritative and canonic Scripture."[13]

Probably for those who will be reading this book the two views that would be held by most are the *Verbal Ple-*

nary view and the *Dynamic Inspiration* view. I personally hold the *Verbal Plenary* view of Scripture.

One's view of the nature of Scripture will greatly influence the manner of her interpretation. The more liberal a person is the less exactitude she uses in her hermeneutic for biblical interpretation.

For instance, the person who accepts *verbal plenary* inspiration will believe that Adam and Eve are real people who actually lived in the Garden of Eden, who sinned, and who were judged by God. Also, he or she will not attempt to change the concept of the Fatherhood of God because the words are clearly male—Father, Son, and He.

At this point we will present the view held by biblical feminists which is *the egalitarian position.*

David Dockery summarizes the egalitarian position as follows:

1. Our existing translations are biased against women (e.g., in 1 Tim. 2:11, "in silence" (KJV) should be translated "quietly" (NEB) or archaic (e.g., and "helpmate for him" does not mean a subordinate helpmate, Gen. 2:18).

2. Although the fact that men and women are partners in fellowship was largely overlooked in patriarchal Israel, even though there is a depatriarchalizing tendency (cf. Song of Solomon; "honor your father and mother"; Judges 4-5). This is continued in the New Testament (Gal. 3:28).

3. Christians shared the cultural attitudes of the first century AD regarding the position of women in a

manner analogous to their attitude toward slavery (cf. Eph. 5:21*ff.* where Paul expresses the reciprocity of marriage in slaves and masters in a similar manner).

4. In Scripture, the understanding and application of revelation is an historical process (cf. Mark 10:2-5). We recognize this is in relation to Christianity's influence on the emancipation of slaves. We must similarly apply this recognition to the issue of women's rightful role today.

5. Paul's letters addressed to specific people with special problems, which called for particular responses which were correct for that situation, must often be translated into underlying general principles if they are to be applicable to us today (e.g., 1 Cor. 14:33-36,40 probably refers to uneducated married women disrupting the order of worship by asking questions; 1 Tim. 2:8-15 may be a response to immature believers teaching heresy in the church).

6. Paul's advice regarding women in the church must be correlated with his description of what women actually did in the early church.

7. We must first be aware of reading twentieth-century nuances into first-century advice (e.g., "head" in 1 Cor. 11:3 is not meant to designate a hierarchy but to suggest women's "source" or "origin" as portrayed in Genesis 2).

8. Those who want to interpret Scripture "literalistically" must be consistent in their approach. If they are, they will see that inadequacy of their position (cf. 1 Cor. 16:20; John 13:14; 1 Tim. 5:23).[14]

In contrast Dockery gives the view held by most conservative Christians, *the traditionalist's position*.

1. No one in biblical Christianity took feminism seriously until it became a dominant theme in our secular humanistic culture.

2. Certainly males predominate in Scripture. The exceptions only prove the rule. Furthermore, Jesus chooses only men as His disciples/apostles and therefore as leaders of His church. To argue for a biblically based feminism is inconsistent with the entire posture of Scripture.

3. The symbolism of the relationship of God to his people (Hosea) and of Christ to His church (Ephesians) demands a male office holder in the church and a male authority in the home. Only in this way is divine authority, dominion, and supremacy adequately portrayed. We are not free to tamper with the biblical imagery without losing some of the mystery.

4. Culture is not happenstance, but prepared by God. Israel with its patriarchal system was peculiarly designed by God as His vehicle of divine truth. Moreover, in the "fullness of time" the gospel came. Thus, Christianity holds that biblical patterns are significant and normative. They reflect the mystery of the divine order. To man is confided the task of ruling, to woman the task of serving.

5. The virgin Mary exemplifies the ideal woman in her voluntary submission and response to the will of God.

6. There is a hierarchy in the created order, each level being given its proper responsibility and

privileges—God, archangels, angels, people, animals, etc. Within the human level woman has been given her place. She is made for man (cf. 1 Cor. 11:9; Gen. 2:18-23). Thus woman is to be deferentially observant in marriage, and man, receptive and responsible. Because of the Fall, men and women have tragically revolted against this creation order.

7. The principles of obedience, submission, and authority are clear in both the OT and NT. The teaching regarding male and female relationships is only one aspect of a larger and necessary reality that extends into the Godhead itself (cf. Christ's obedience and submission to the Father and the Holy Spirit's subordination to the Son).[15]

Incorrect Interpretations

Interpretation is very important. Faulty reasoning and the "building of straw men," and then knocking them down, results in false conclusions. A false assumption of what biblical conservatives believe is unfortunate. For instance, some incorrect interpretations biblical feminists have built are the following:

1. *Submission Implies Inferiority.*

Phyliss Trible, called by fellow Old Testament scholar Walter Brueggemann the decisive voice in the interpretation of biblical literature, argues against the idea that the "biblical texts imply inferiority or subordination of the woman because she was created second," in her interpretation of Genesis 2-3.[16]

Indeed the woman was placed in a position of submission, *but it was never implied that submission means infe-*

riority. Submission simply means being "under" the authority of another. Biblical submission indicates one equal willingly placing himself or herself under the authority of another equal. Submission is the woman's God-assigned role. In His wisdom God knew she needed the leadership and protection of the male. He had created her with these needs. Any insinuation of inferiority originates from man's sinful, self-seeking nature. Here is where we must correctly divide between a biblical principle and a sin-related abuse.

2. *The Woman Bears Greater Responsibility for Sin.*

Trible assumes that those who teach "that the woman was the deceived being in the transgression (1 Tim. 2:14) believe that she bears greater responsibility for sin."

As a woman I am saddened that it was a woman who was deceived and sinned first, but we cannot deny that fact if we believe the Bible is true. However, it is *not* correct that biblical conservatives believe the woman bears greater responsibility for sin. This is a "straw man." I believe that by this incorrect interpretation a great truth is overlooked.

In fact the Bible states, "As in *Adam* all die . . . ." This passage doesn't even mention Eve. Yes, Eve sinned first. Yes, Eve was deceived, but Adam was her head. She was *under his* authority—therefore he was accountable for her actions. Oh, she was guilty; she was judged, but *he* was also accountable for her actions.

But praise God, "As in *Adam* all die, even so in Christ shall all be made alive." Christ was the second Adam from above. He willingly bore our sins.

3. *"Head" Means Source Instead of Ruler.*

The *headship* of the man is the basic concept of functional order for men and women that the *biblical feminist* tries to avoid.

Biblical feminists try to prove that "head" does not mean ruler but instead "source." They illustrate their interpretation from Colossians 2:9-10 which speaks of Christ, "For in him dwelleth all the fulness of the Godhead bodily. And ye are complete in him, which is the head of all principality and power" (KJV). They then state that "head" here obviously means "source," and that we have been made one with that source, not subject to it.

They also refer to Ephesians 1:22 where it declares that God has given Him headship over "all things to the church." They ask the question, "What is in subjection?" The answer, "not the body but the world which is under his feet." Sometimes this is linked to Genesis 3:15.

"Head," they say, as employed metaphorically in the New Testament, speaks in reference to a dynamic, living unity, a one-flesh relationship. The head of the church is not its ruler but its source of life, they say. *Kephalē* is used almost synonymously with *archē* (beginning). Thus, they feel, *kephalē* implies what *archē* does—that fountainhead or the headwaters of a river are indicated, and hence, source.

They also say that Christ is our "head" in the sense that He is the first fruits of the dead (see 1 Cor. 15:20).

There is also an effort to disprove the concepts of headship and submission in regard to husbands and wives. Yes, they say, Christian wives are to submit to their husbands as the church submits to Christ. Husbands then are not told to pattern their headship after Christ in His rulership of the universe but rather to follow His example of self-giving oneness with His body.

Granted that "head" can in some instances also mean "source," that does not eliminate that sometimes it can mean "ruler." In moving heaven and earth to prove their position of mutual leadership, Christian feminists have also effectively "proven" that the Church is not subject to Christ—that He is not the ruler over His body, only one with it.

Saying that husbands "are to follow Christ's example of self-giving oneness with His body, the Church," does not prove that the wife is not to be in submission to her husband or that Christ is not the ruler of His body, the Church.

The head is joined to and is one with the human body, but it nevertheless contains the brain which is the control-center of the body. The brain will not give any direction that will harm any other part of the body, for it is one with the body. So Christ is the head of His body, the Church. He not only is the source of life for the Church, but He is Lord—or Ruler—of the Church.

So the husband is "over" his wife, though he is one with her. If he is led by the Spirit, he will do nothing to harm her. He will be a "covering" or protection for her because of His abundant love for her. He is supposed to be a picture of Christ to his wife.

A large number of biblical feminists see a contradiction

between the submission of the woman and the headship of the man. There is no contradiction if *sin-related abuses* are eliminated—evidenced by a spirit of servanthood in the man and a spirit of respect in the woman. We cannot change God's *functional order* to correct abuses.

Mutual Submission

The biblical feminist goes to great lengths to negate the submission of wives to husbands. One way they try to do this is by quoting verses about what they call *mutual submission*. One such verse is in Ephesians 5:21, "Submitting yourselves one to another in the fear of God." However, it is followed in verse 22 by this command, "Wives, submit yourselves unto your husbands, as unto the Lord." Though seemingly contradictory, they are not. The injunction to submit *mutually* to one another becomes a buffer against the *abuse* of headship.

Another passage deals with *mutual* submission in the Church. First Peter 5:2 exhorts the elders to willingly take the *oversight* or leadership, not for money but of a ready mind. In verse 3 he warns them against *over*ruling. "Neither as being lords [overruling] over God's heritage, but being examples to the flock."

Then in verse 5 he admonishes the younger to submit to the elder. That is immediately followed by a command to "be subject one to another, and be clothed with humility: for God resisteth the proud, and giveth grace to the humble." God through Peter is obviously warning against the abuse of even God-ordained authority. We must mutually "give up our rights" in all humility.

Anyone who thinks the admonition to be *mutually* submissive negates the commands to God's delegated authorities clearly misunderstands the Scriptures.

Susan Foh explains these two complementary concepts this way:

> The woman as her husband's helper is to submit to him in a way that he does not submit to her. The requirement for the wife is characterized by submission; for the husband it is characterized by love. The requirements are not the same.
>
> The difference is made sure in Ephesians 5:31. The woman should fear or *reverence* her husband, and he is to *love* her. The reverse cannot be said. In addition, the comparison with Christ and the church cannot be reversed. Christ served the church and the church serves Christ, just as there is *mutual service* between husband and wife.
>
> Yet, Christ's authority over the church is in no way undermined by His self-giving love. Likewise for all the mutuality between husband and wife, he remains her head and has authority over her.[17]

Sin-Related Abuses

Some men, sadly even some Christian men, have implied the woman's inferiority. Some have wrongly interpreted their role of headship and become harsh and dictatorial. But this is a *sin*-related abuse, not the fault of the God-given principle.

As we have stated, Jesus demonstrated that the principle of submission did not imply inferiority. He was and is of equal *worth* but had a different *function*. He was in submission to His Father but was not inferior.

It is particularly misleading when Christian men have misused and abused their roles because God intended to demonstrate through Spirit-filled men how He wanted His servant-leader to function.

Man-made Customs

Customs vary from age to age and from culture to culture. There are customs related to modesty, to masculinity, and to manners, as well as many other subjects. In our culture it is considered rude to belch after you eat, but it is a sign of delight and satisfaction in Taiwan. In the Middle East a woman must cover her shoulders lest she be thought to be provocative. Twenty years ago in this country a man was considered "henpecked" if he helped with the dishes or changed diapers. These are culture-related customs, not great underlying principles from the Word of God.

A problem arises when customs and principles are so closely joined that it becomes difficult to separate them. Nevertheless, customs should not be lightly or suddenly laid aside. Someone has said, "Don't be the first by whom the new is tried or the last by whom the old is laid aside."

An example of a custom and a biblical principle being closely joined together is the length of hair for men and women. The Bible clearly states that even nature teaches that it is a shame for a man to have long hair (1 Cor. 11:14). Then it follows in verse 15 that, "if a woman have long hair, it is a glory to her." I believe this principle with all my heart. There should be a definite difference in the length of hair of men and women. The latter part of verse 15 states, "for hair is given her for a covering." I believe that a woman's *longer* hair symbolizes that she is *under* male authority.

Now the Bible doesn't say how long is long and how short is short. Customs vary from culture to culture and age to age. But in all cultures and at all times there should be a difference in the appearance of men and women. Their hair is one distinguishing factor. A woman's hair is to be longer. God doesn't want any she-men or he-women. He is not in favor of the unisex movement. Those who are tend to do away with the distinction between male and female hair styles.

We must have God's wisdom to be able to discern between man-made customs and biblical principles. But customs may change. In the 1960s some Christians thought it was sinful for a man's hair to go over his ears or touch his collar. Some of us were disturbed over our children conforming to the cultural change. Now men's hair styles are shorter. Right when we were accepting a fuller look, custom dictated, "Let's give the guys a skinned look." Whereas longer hair was a symbol of rebellion in the 1960s, the *skinhead* is a sign of rebellion in the 1980s.

Customs change. Hairstyles change. Fashions change. But God's written Word is the same, and it is just as true now as it was when it was originally inspired. And Jesus Christ, the living Word, is "the same yesterday, and to day, and for ever." (Heb. 13:8).

Summary

In summary, the secret to a godly woman's influence is "living *under* authority." Jesus gave great recognition for the faith of the centurion who asked Him to heal his servant. This army officer confessed he was not worthy for Jesus to come to his house; but if He would only speak the word, his servant would be healed.

The centurion declared, "For I am a man under authority, having soldiers under me: and I say to this man, Go, and he goeth; and to another, Come, and he cometh; and to my servant, Do this, and he doeth it" (Matt. 8:9). Jesus marveled and told those with him, ". . . I have not found so great faith, no, not in Israel" (Matt. 8:10).

What was the secret of the centurion's faith? Why did Jesus commend him? He understood the principle of "living *under* authority." This principle works in every area of life. His life as a soldier operated upon this principle every day. He knew that those who have authority are those who live *under* authority.

He surmised that the spiritual world must work on the same principle. He had observed that Jesus had authority over sickness, so he knew that Jesus was a man who lived under spiritual authority. Even so, if we as women understand the principle of "living *under* authority," we will be women of incomparable faith and will exercise godly authority. But we will not have to demand our rights. Others will recognize this authority and follow the leadership of one who is "living *under* authority."

Godly authority does not always involve having the number-one position. Many times a person with another position may have even greater ability in some areas than the head person. If he or she is not mainly interested in getting the credit and gaining recognition, even more significant influence can be gained.

For instance, a wife can have tremendous influence on her husband's decisions if she is wise in her counsel and if she has a submissive spirit. She may not be given public recognition for her ideas, but God has indeed promised an appropriate recognition for her ideas. Proverbs 31:28 says that, "Her children arise up and call her blessed; her husband also and he praiseth her."

I believe, in the long run, a wife can have more influence and know more true success in a supportive position to make her husband successful than if she tries to succeed in her own separate career.

> Two are better than one; because they have a good reward for their labour. For if they fall, the one will lift up his fellow; but woe to him that is alone when he falleth; for he hath not another to help him up. Again, if two lie together, then they have heat: but how can one be warm alone? And if one prevail against him, two shall withstand him, and a threefold cord is not quickly broken (Eccl. 2:9-12).

I believe the third part of the cord that binds them together is God's precious Holy Spirit.

Thank God, we don't have to experience forlorn emptiness as we look back on the lives we have lived. We can know true freedom, hope, joy, and contentment if we live under God's principle of authority.

Esther risked her life to fall down before the king to intercede for the lives of her people. Because he saw in her a godly, submissive spirit, he held out the golden scepter toward her. "So Esther arose, and stood before the king" (Esther 8:4).

So should we fall before our Heavenly King in quiet submission, seeking His will for our lives. In so doing God will reach out His loving hand of mercy towards us and say, "Arise, my daughter. Stand before Me, and I will grant you your request."

Notes

PART I A WOMAN'S INFLUENCE

1. Copyright © 1949 by Singspiration Music/ASCAP. Renewed 1979. All rights reserved. Used by permission of the Benson Company, Nashville, Tennessee.

2. C. Austin Miles, "Submission" (The Rodeheaver Co., Copyright renewal 1962). Used by permission.

PART II SPHERES OF INFLUENCE – YIELDED TO THE LORDSHIP OF CHRIST

1. Larry Christenson, *The Christian Family* (Minneapolis, MN: Bethany Fellowship, 1970), p. 32-33.

2. Ibid., p. 43.

3. Ibid., p. 42.

PART III WOMEN IN MINISTRY

1. Catherine Allen, *A Century to Celebrate, History of Woman's Missionary Union* (Birmingham, AL: New Hope Press, 1987), p. 148.

2. Ibid., p. 46.

3. Ibid., Chapter 3.

4. Ibid., p. 330.

5. Mrs. Howard Taylor, *The Triumph of John and Betty Stam* (Chicago: Moody Press, 1935), pp. 141,143.

6. Ethel Mary Baldwin and David V. Benson, *Henrietta Mears and How She Did It!* (Glendale, CA: Regal Books, 1966).

PART IV WOMAN'S ROLE TODAY

1. *Revolution: Tomorrow Is Now,* Chapter Workbook, Compiled by Mary Samis, Tish Sommers, Marjorie Suelzle, and Nan Wood (Washington, D.C.: National Organization for Women, 1973), p. 18.

2. Tim LaHaye, *The Battle for the Mind* (Old Tappan, New Jersey: Fleming H. Revell Co., 1980), p. 27.

3. Ibid., p. 57.

4. *Humanist Manifestos I and II* (Buffalo, NY: Prometheus Books, 1973), p. 16.

5. Ibid., p. 17.

6. Ibid., p. 21.

7. *The Wall Street Journal,* "The Cost of Equality," Jan. 14, 1980 (Vol. LXV, No. 9).

8. Ibid.

9. Ibid.

10. *The Commercial Appeal,* Memphis, Tennessee, July 25, 1987.

11. Norman L. Geisler and William Nix, *A General Introduction to the Bible* (Chicago: Moody Press, 1968), pp. 46-47.

12. Ibid., p. 45.

13. Ibid., pp. 46-47.

14. R. K. Johnstone, "The Role of Women in the Church and Home," p. 237. Quoted in "The Role of Women in Worship and Ministry: Some Hermeneutical Questions," *Criswell Theological Review,* Vol. I, No. 2, Spring 1987, p. 379.

15. Ibid., p. 239.

16. Phyllis Trible, "Depatriarchalizing," pp. 35-42, and *Rhetoric of Human Sexuality,* see pp. 72-143.

17. Susan T. Foh, *Women and the Word of God* (Presbyterian Reformed Publishing Co., 1979), p. 200.